101
MOMENTS
IN THE
PRESENCE OF GOD

INSPIRING THOUGHTS
FOR EVERYDAY LIVING

RICK HAMLIN

Executive Editor, *Guideposts* Magazine

Guideposts

New York

101 Moments in the Presence of God

Published by Guideposts Books & Inspirational Media
110 William Street
New York, New York 10038
Guideposts.org

Acknowledgments

Every attempt has been made to credit the sources of copyrighted material used in this book. If any such acknowledgment has been inadvertently omitted or miscredited, receipt of such information would be appreciated.

All Scripture quotations, unless otherwise noted, are taken from *The King James Version of the Bible*.

Scripture quotations marked (NIV) are taken from *The Holy Bible, New International Version*. Copyright © 1973, 1978, 1984 International Bible Society. Used by permission of Zondervan Bible Publishers.

Scripture quotations marked (RSV) are taken from the *Revised Standard Version of the Bible*. Copyright © 1946, 1952, 1971 by Division of Christian Education of the National Council of Churches of Christ in the U.S.A. Used by permission.

Edited by Jill Jones
Cover and interior design by Müllerhaus
Typeset by Aptara, Inc.

Printed and bound in the United States of America
10 9 8 7 6 5 4

INTRODUCTION

My wife, Carol, has gotten all too used to that look that comes over my face at certain moments, when something she or the kids have done has struck me. "Are you going to turn this into a devotion?" she'll say.

For instance, there was that handmade beaded bracelet she started wearing one spring. I couldn't quite gather why she always had it on. Was this some new fashion statement? No, Carol explained, a friend was suffering a serious bout of depression. She had made the bracelet for Carol as part of her therapy. "Every time I look at it, I remember to pray for her," Carol said.

Then one day it was gone. "Where's that bracelet?" I asked.

"I've got something better," she said.

"What's that?"

"A friend who's well."

Or I can recall a Father's Day when I took our younger son, Timothy, to church, then to his baseball game. We bought sodas and enchiladas from the woman who cooks them in the park. At home I scanned the newspaper, took a nap, helped Tim with some homework. After dinner I read to him and he said his prayers. Just before I kissed him good night, I asked, "So Tim, what did you give me for Father's Day?"

"A perfect day," he said. He did.

I've found inspiration for devotions in places I never expected. Like in the trunk of the ancient Volvo Mom and Dad gave us when they finally bought a new one. Dad had left an old carpet sample in the trunk. *What on earth for?* I wondered. That winter a storm buried the car under eighteen inches of snow. I managed to shovel most of it off, but the car couldn't get any traction on the ice. Then I remembered that carpet sample. I took it out of the trunk and stuck it under the tires. Wouldn't you know? It worked like a dream—a gift from heaven.

A devotion starts with a Bible verse and ends with a prayer, but what makes it compelling is how it shows God at work in the everyday moments. It's a beaded bracelet that leads to an answered prayer, a child's remark at bedtime, a carpet sample in the back of a car.

Almost two thousand years ago, two of Jesus' followers were walking to the village of Emmaus when they were joined by a stranger. They couldn't believe he didn't know what had happened, how the man they thought was the Messiah was crucified and then appeared to some of the women in their group. The stranger spoke wisely and passionately to them, but not until they sat with him and broke bread did they recognize that he was their risen Lord.

That's what a devotion feels like. That moment when I get a glimpse of God's presence. Not that God's ever been far away. All I needed to do was look. All I needed to be was aware.

—Rick Hamlin

ONE SIMPLE VERB

Make a joyful noise unto the Lord, all ye lands.
—PSALM 100:1

The "Rejoice" banner goes up on New Year's Day at my mom and dad's home. It usually hangs over the garage, the colorful letters on a white background reminding the neighbors to rejoice. Something of a historical artifact, it made its first appearance on January 1, 1983, carried by two Boy Scouts down Colorado Boulevard before a million people in Pasadena in that year's Rose Parade—what we always refer to as "Dad's parade."

That was when Dad was president of the Tournament of Roses, the volunteer organization that runs the Rose Parade and the Rose Bowl. He and Mom traveled across the country, meeting the bands that would march in the parade and the civic groups that would sponsor floats. They ate at pancake breakfast fundraisers, shook hands with mayors and boosters, marched in other parades, and cheered through Pac Ten/Big Ten football games. In preparation, Dad crowned a Rose queen and selected a grand marshal. But his biggest challenge was to come up with a theme for the parade.

I can remember some of the rejects: "Faith and Family," "Faith, Hope, and Love," "Faith and Enterprise" (somehow I could never see that on a banner carried down Colorado Boulevard). Clearly Dad was trying to find the right message to help people celebrate the New Year. "It should have meaning for everybody," he said.

What Dad finally settled on was a simple verb, one that appears a couple of hundred times in the Bible. It was on the banner and the floats and in the band music, and it was the word he repeated that sunny morning as he waved from the horse-drawn, flower-covered carriage that led the parade.

"Rejoice."

What a way to greet the New Year!

Lord, on this New Year's Day, I rejoice in the world You made.

||||||||||||||||||||||||||||||||||||||||||||||||||||||||||||||||||||||||||||||||||||||||||||||||||||||||||||||||||||||

LOOKING FORWARD

He shall grow up before him as a tender plant,
and as a root out of a dry ground….
—ISAIAH 53:2

There's an old patch of wood that we keep unpainted in our back room near the storage cabinets.

The dates and names start at the bottom, a little more than three feet above the ground, in childish handwriting. The writing becomes more secure when the names rise higher, and it's positively mature well above five feet. There's William on 9-12-99 and then William a foot higher on 5-10-03. Timothy seems to make the same rapid progress a little behind his older brother. Mom and Dad never seem to change. I never rise above five feet eleven inches, but the boys leapfrog over each other until you see them leap above their mother—a strong black line to mark the milestone—and then they rise above their father, leaving him in the dust.

Then the writing stops—no more updates; no need for more. But the old marks are still there, and I can glance at them when I'm getting down the gardening shears or looking for a screwdriver. My friend Tib reminds me that the one prayer God never answers is "Please, let nothing change." When I cling too tightly to the past, I can look at this record of how the boys grew until they towered over me. So many answers to prayer in indelible ink. Someday we'll have to move from this home, but I hope the new owners can make their own marks of progress along the wood.

Lord, let me look forward, always remembering the love that has been with me all along.

‖‖

MOUSE EARS

They have ears, but they hear not….
—PSALM 115:6

It began with the mouse in the wall behind our bed. Quiet during the day, the creature liked to scratch on the plaster at 1:00 AM or 2:00 AM, and the sound resonated down the wall, making it impossible to sleep. We asked our cat, Fred the Fearless Hunter, to investigate the fine-line cracks in the plaster in hopes that he'd sniff out a way to trap our tormentor or scare it away. No such luck. I didn't want to put out poison or a glue trap. "Why don't you try one of those machines that make a high-pitched buzzing sound?" a friend suggested. "No one can hear it but a mouse, and it'll send it away."

I went off to the hardware store and bought the buzzing apparatus for $19.95, plugged it in, and turned it on. Fred investigated it, shrugged, and ambled off. My wife admired its size and shape. "What about that loud noise?" I said.

"What noise?" Carol asked.

"That buzzing sound," I said. "Doesn't that bother you?"

She had no idea what I was talking about and neither did our son Tim. Turns out I had to wait until the advanced age of fifty-four to discover that I have the hearing of a mouse.

We found a corner of the room to put the machine where it didn't bother me too much, but it bothered the mouse enough that it buzzed off for good. As for my extrasensory hearing? It doesn't seem to do me much good. But it does make me laugh to know that I've got mouse ears.

Thank You, God, for the many gifts You give me.
May I use them to the best of my ability.

##########

STICK WITH IT!

We must through much tribulation enter into
the kingdom of God.
—ACTS 14:22

I've begun to call it Good Idea Hill.

It's the least favorite part of my usual morning run. I jog through our neighborhood, past the school where the teachers are just arriving, past the church and the playground, into the park where, depending on the season, the heather, the azaleas, the dogwood, the peonies, the roses, the daylilies, the poppies, the chrysanthemums bloom. I come around the path to the wide lawn where there's always a jogger or a walker to say good morning to.

But then comes the big hill, a long, slow rise on an asphalt road. Sure, there are old elm trees and a blush of impatiens and a view across the Hudson River if I look, but my eyes get glued to the ground and I start thinking, *I'm not going to make it.*

Oddly enough, though, as I push through my fatigue, a lighter stream of thought comes through, telling me, *You should call so-and-so* or *Write a note to such-and-such* or *You should buy mom X for her birthday.* It's a time when my imagination starts spinning with good ideas. I suppose I could have stumbled on them lying in bed, getting an extra half-hour of sleep, but I wouldn't count on it. The combination of endorphins, sunshine, effort, and fatigue somehow delivers—and at just the moment when I'm ready to give up. It's like that moment in prayer when you don't think you have anything left to say and you can't imagine what God has to say to you; somehow, prayer happens.

So whatever you're doing, whatever challenges you're facing, stick with the hills. They give back.

Lord, I will press on and persevere even at those times that are especially tough, because that's often when I come to know You.

||||||||||||||||||||||||||||||||||||||||||||||||||||||||||||||||||||||||||||||||||||||||||||||||||||||||||||

HEALING IN A CAT'S PURR

Heal me, O Lord, and I shall be healed; save me,
and I shall be saved....
—JEREMIAH 17:14

A friend told me that the purring of cats has a healing power. I wasn't so sure. Perhaps it's because our cat, a large Maine coon mix that was rescued from the subway platform, is a less-than-perfect pet. Fred won't sit in my lap for more than thirty seconds and never voluntarily. He likes to wake us up at 6:00 AM for his breakfast, even when there's food still in the bowl. He claws at the sofa. He unloads cat hair in remarkable quantities (you could knit a sweater from the stuff we collect). Fortunately, he's good at purring.

Take out his brush, he purrs. Sit next to him on the bed, he purrs. Scratch him on the flat part of his nose, he purrs so loud I think the neighbors can hear. That his purring can be healing was revealed to me the other night.

It was 3:00 AM, and I wasn't sleeping well. Too many things were going through my mind. I was doing my best to pray through the worries—give them back to God—without much success.

Then Fred leaped up on the bed and meowed. "No, Fred," I whispered, "it's not time for breakfast." He lay down next to my head, his tail twitching, and purred, an incredibly loud, comforting, satisfying sound. It turned out to be just what I needed. I scratched him on the forehead and I'm not sure where the worries went, but the next time I woke up it was 6:10 AM. Fred was letting me know he was hungry.

"Thanks for the extra ten minutes, pal," I told him. And for the purring!

God, You have so many ways of giving me
Your healing touch.

A FRONT ROW SEAT

Worship the Lord in the beauty of holiness.
—I CHRONICLES 16:29

It used to embarrass me to no end when Dad marched Mom and all four of us kids down the center aisle at church to sit in the front pew—granted, we were never on time. And as I was growing up, nobody ever sat up there. Nobody. The church could be packed to the gills and the last seat anybody took was in the front pew. Out of excessive humility or a fear of being blasted out of their seats, everybody else filled up the back first.

In our teen years we couldn't crane our heads around, without being completely obvious, to see some girlfriend three rows back. If we were tuckered out from a Saturday night party, we couldn't sneak in on the side. There we were, right up in front. "Why do we sit here?" I asked Dad.

"It's easier to feel like I'm part of the service," he said to my bewilderment.

I could never figure it out and I didn't really have to. During most of my adulthood I've sung in choirs or shepherded the Sunday school kids, and that meant never sitting in front. But one day when there was no choir and no Sunday school, my wife and I wandered into church early and sat in front for a change. I wasn't sure I liked it. I couldn't swivel around to see who was bellowing on that opening hymn or who was away on vacation. But it was easier to concentrate on the sermon, and during the prayers, I could feel the congregation right behind me. It was as though they were holding me up, keeping me going.

I don't know where you usually sit in church, but I'd recommend the front row from time to time. You'll feel the support of the congregation behind you and know just why you're there.

Keep me, Lord, in this front-row seat with the perfect view of Your creation.

||||||||||||||||||||||||||||||||||||||||||||||||||||||||||||||||||||||||||||||||||||||||||||||||||||||||||

THE POWER OF SONG

Praise him with the sound of the trumpet:
praise him with the psaltery and harp.
—PSALM 150:3

I used to wonder why my parents and their friends went into such exaggerated paroxysms of enjoyment whenever they heard big-band tunes like "String of Pearls" or "Sing, Sing, Sing." Not that I didn't like them myself—it's just that what I heard didn't fully explain the tear in the eye, the elbow in the ribs, or the infectious foot-tapping that came over anyone who had been in their late teens when they first heard those tunes.

Then not long ago I was listening to the car radio and I was suddenly transported back to my own late teens. All at once I was driving the family station wagon over a mustard-drenched hill near San Francisco on a rainy Easter weekend. The Golden Gate Bridge was in the background, high school graduation was in the foreground, and I felt the rich thrill of possibilities ahead of me as Roberta Flack sang "Killing Me Softly with His Song."

That's what music will do—take you back to former days. It's the pleasure I find when I sing hymns. When I hear "The

Church's One Foundation," I'm reminded of the small gathering of family and friends that sang it at our wedding. "Holy, Holy, Holy" takes me back to my boyhood church and the devotion of our tireless organist transposing the last verse up a half step. With "Onward Christian Soldiers," I recall the memorial service for a dear friend who won a valiant spiritual battle in her losing war against cancer.

In church we use the phrase "a cloud of witnesses" to describe the believers who have preceded us and whom we will follow. They hover about me in familiar songs.

I praise You, Lord, for the gift of music.

CONSTANT SCENES OF FORGIVENESS

Who can understand his errors?
cleanse thou me from secret faults.
—PSALM 19:12

I crammed my cereal bowl, spoon, and juice glass into the overcrowded dishwasher, thinking to myself, *Carol is sure going to have trouble fitting in her dishes when she has breakfast.*

I brushed my teeth, picked up my bag, and then went back into the kitchen to kiss her before heading out to work. To my surprise, she was unloading the dishwasher.

"I just put my dirty dishes in there," I warned her.

"But these dishes are already clean," she said. "I turned on the dishwasher after dinner last night."

"But," I stammered, "the door was unlatched this morning…"

"I opened it before I went to bed," she said. "I took out a glass."

"My breakfast dishes aren't clean."

"Which ones are they?"

I peered into the upper rack. "Here," I said. "This bowl…and this juice glass."

"What about your spoon?" she asked.

"It's on the bottom rack." I looked at all the spoons in there. No way would I be able to pick out the one that was slightly dirty.

"I'll find it," she said.

"Okay." I leaned over to kiss her. "I'll be home for dinner."

She kissed my cheek back. "See you later."

A marriage is founded on constant scenes of forgiveness. Even for husbands who don't notice that they're putting a dirty cereal bowl, juice glass, and spoon in a completely clean dishwasher.

Forgive me for all my faults, Lord.
You more than anyone know what they are.

THE WORLD OF BOOKS

Write the vision, and make it plain upon tables,
that he may run that readeth it.
—HABAKKUK 2:2

Anna Karenina is a big book—840 pages in my hardcover edition—and it weighs a couple of pounds. It's a lot to lug around, but the best opportunity I have for reading is going from place to place. So I took Tolstoy's novel everywhere with me. I read it on the subway and the bus. I read it on the treadmill at the gym. I confess I even read it walking to work (without bumping into anyone).

But when I wasn't reading it, the characters were still with me. There was a dark-haired woman who looked just like Anna coming out of Lord and Taylor. The dashing Vronsky strolled right out of a brokerage on Fifth Avenue, walking down the avenue like he owned the place. At the farmer's market in Union Square, I was sure I spotted the earnest farmer Levin. He wore a floppy leather hat, a bemused expression, and he was carrying a bag of corn.

And then there were all the people I met who were great fans of the book. One man stopped me on the street and asked, "How do you like it?" Another time, I was reading the novel on the bus when I heard a woman's voice, "Where are you?" I looked up. "Has Levin proposed to Kitty yet?" she asked.

"He's proposed once," I said, "but I'm waiting for him to do it again."

Many would say that reading a book is a solitary activity. Perhaps, but I don't think a reader can ever be lonely. The best books—whether it's Tolstoy or the Bible—open us up to a whole world. Especially on the streets of New York City.

I give thanks for the world of books, Lord.

WINGS AND ROOTS

A wise son maketh a glad father....
—PROVERBS 10:1

A friend of mine claims that it's the job of a parent to give a child both roots and wings. Well, when Timothy went off to college and Carol and I no longer had any boys at home, I was worried that maybe we'd overdone it in the wings department.

I mean, for the first week Tim didn't even call, and after that we'd get only nuggets: He loved his classes, he had great friends, he was playing Frisbee on the lawn and working hard. But in my empty-nest stage, I kept wondering: Didn't he miss us even a little? Didn't he miss our fall rituals, like shopping for apples at the green market, going to a Columbia football game, carving a jack-o'-lantern, planting the spring bulbs? Every November we'd put in tulip bulbs and daffodils and crocuses. Now I'd have to do it on my own.

"I'm glad Tim's happy," I'd say in my prayers, "but fall feels empty without him."

Then one day I came home from work and Carol said, "There's a package for you on the dining room table." A sizable cardboard box from some unknown address, it smelled faintly of damp earth. I opened it. On top were an order form and a card. "Happy Father's Day a little late," it said. "Love, Tim." There in the box were bulbs—spring bulbs to plant in the autumn.

"What a great present, Tim," I told him on the phone. "I'm glad you didn't forget."

"Sure, Dad," he said. Wings and roots: It takes both.

May my children remember where they're from
as they spread their wings and fly.

‖‖

THE SUPPORT OF FRIENDS

Two are better than one....
—ECCLESIASTES 4:9

The jog I take a couple of times a week from our house to the park, down through the Heather Garden and up around the museum—oh, that hill—doesn't seem to get any easier. When I think of the hundreds of times I've done this short run, I don't see why it should be such a challenge, but in the morning when I punch the alarm clock and pull on my sweatpants, it's as though I'm about to climb Mount Everest. The first few yards out of the driveway and up to the corner mailbox are excruciating.

Then something happens. I pass a neighbor walking her dogs and wish her good morning. I see a friend taking his two children to school and marvel at how tall they've grown. I notice the marigolds and dahlias that some intrepid urban gardener has planted beneath the sycamores. I wave to a hearty trio of walkers coming down the hill I'm about to climb. "Keep it up," we tell one another. Just when I don't think I'm going to make it, I hear footsteps behind me. "Hey, stranger," a voice says. It's Michael, one of the neighborhood dads I've hardly seen since our kids graduated from Little League. "Can I join you?"

We do the loop around the museum and take in an extra loop for good measure, something I would have never done without his encouragement. We stop at the playground for a few pull-ups.

"How was your run?" my wife Carol asks when I get home.

"Great," I say. "I caught up with the neighborhood." They're the ones who keep me in shape. You can always travel faster and farther when you're with friends.

I thank You, God, for the friends who give me encouragement and help me on my way.

||||||||||||||||||||||||||||||||||||||||||||||||||||||||||||||||||||||||||

LENGTHENING SHADOWS

Cast me not off in the time of old age;
forsake me not when my strength faileth.
—PSALM 71:9

My father gets around with a walker these days, and he doesn't get around much. But he was there when the whole clan—twenty and counting—gathered for a week at the beach, staying at a rental on the sand. We sailed, we surfed, we rode bikes on the boardwalk, swam out to the buoy, and kayaked in the bay. Dad seemed to enjoy having everybody together, but even from under the umbrella on the porch, he got frustrated at not being able to do half of what he once could.

Late one afternoon I suggested a walk. "I'm not sure how I can do it with this walker on the sand," he said.

"Let's try," I said. "You can hold my hand if you need to."

He made his way down the beach, leaning on the walker or me. We stopped to watch some sailors bring their boats to shore and take down their sails. "Hey, Mr. Hamlin!" one of the guys called. "How are you doing?"

"Just fine," he said, his hands on the walker.

We trudged back next to the water, choosing the hard sand. A pelican dipped past us and plunged into the bay, picking up dinner. A kayak cut across the smooth water, a fish leaping in its wake. The shadows of the palms lengthened across the sand in front of us. "The shadows lengthen," Dad observed.

They do, I thought. The years go by, and you don't know where they went. Age brings its struggles. But at the end of the day there are still beauties to be found in a setting sun and a slow walk on the beach, father and son.

All those years my father took care of me, Lord,
may I now take good care of him.

<hr>

HAPPILY LOST

He that findeth his life shall lose it: and he that loseth
his life for my sake shall find it.
—MATTHEW 10:39

I'm sitting on a park bench, reading a book while the butterflies hover over a stalk of hollyhocks and then flutter to the daylilies bending on their stems. I've come to this bench as I often do on a Saturday to escape the phone and the computer and the bills that need to be paid. I even make a point of not taking a watch. It's my sort of "staycation"—a way of getting away without going far at all.

All of a sudden my calm is interrupted by a boy, about three years old, who dashes along the path and then ducks behind a hedge. "I'm hiding!" he calls to his mother, who's pushing an empty stroller along the path behind him. "You can't see me!" he yells, his blond cowlick rising over the shrubbery like a duck's tail.

Of course she can see him and so can I. But I know just how he feels, the two of us hiding from the world. I sit on my park bench, close my eyes, and feel far away from the stresses that put me off balance and make me less than the person I want to be, until I remember Whose I am and what's really important in my life.

The boy pops up from behind the hedge and greets his mother in a fit of giggles. "You found me!" he exclaims.

"I did!" she says, giving him a hug.

I watch them go and then get up from my bench, glad of my escape. Happy to be lost for a while just so I, too, can be found.

Lord, I lose myself today so that You can find me.

<hr/>

NO NEED TO WORRY

Take therefore no thought for the morrow: for the morrow shall take thought for the things of itself....
—MATTHEW 6:34

On a day when I was worrying too much about money—the immensity of college tuitions occupying too much of my brain—I stepped away from the computer and picked up an old family photo album.

There was a picture of William's pirate birthday party when he was five, his classmates dressed in eye patches and bandannas, brandishing plastic swords and searching for buried treasure. There was a shot of Timothy in white with a silver halo circling his blond head, the perfect angel dressed for the Christmas pageant. There were photos of the boys in their baseball uniforms and snapshots of us at picnics in friends' backyards—that was me pushing Tim in a swing, both of us laughing so hard you could see our tonsils. My eye lingered at the one of Carol and me sitting in beach chairs, the boys splashing in the bay, neither of us with a care in the world....

Until I remembered all the things I worried about that day at the beach, like how would we ever afford nursery school and would Timothy ever learn his colors and would William please get a base hit at least once. In fact, if I looked closely at the photos, I could recall worries that had plagued me at every moment—all the way back to the proud moment I first held William in my arms.

I closed the album and went back to the computer. *See*, I told myself, *you got through that just fine. You'll get through this too.*

Lord, I promise not to let worries for tomorrow
rob me of the pleasures of this day.

||||||||||||||||||||||||||||||||||||||||||||||||||||||||||||||||||||||||||||||||

GUITAR HERO

The blessing of the Lord was upon all that
he had in the house, and in the field.
—GENESIS 39:5

Not long ago my wife Carol and I were visiting twenty-one-year-old William at his college for Parents Weekend.

"Have you seen Guitar Hero?" he asked. No, we hadn't...and I wasn't sure whether it was a movie, TV show, or computer game.

"It's a computer game, Dad," Will said. "Here, try it." He logged on to his laptop and handed me a fake plastic guitar.

"What am I supposed to do with this?"

"You play it," he said. "Just follow the directions on the computer."

I slung the guitar over my shoulder and, staring at the screen, attempted to follow an obstacle course of signals as I played "Sunshine of My Love"—an easy one, my son assured me. It took all my concentration to change chords and strum at the right times, bouncing on the balls of my feet.

A couple of weeks later, Timothy, our younger son, exclaimed, "Dad, did you know you're on Will's Facebook page?" There I was, a skinny, gray-haired wannabe rock star, biting his lip and bouncing out of his sneakers.

"My dad, Guitar Hero," Will had written.

To honor your father and mother can take many different forms these days. Being called a hero—even teasingly—on Facebook is fine by me.

Lord, give me the courage to try the unfamiliar.

||||||||||||||||||||||||||||||||||||||||||||||||||||||||||||||||||||||||||||||||||||||

STRETCHES AND PRAYERS

I have called daily upon thee, I have stretched out
my hands unto thee.
—PSALM 88:9

There's always some know-it-all at the gym who will be a spoilsport no matter what. Just the other day I was on the floor, going through a series of stretches, working out the kinks in my back, thighs, calves, and hamstrings, and, of course, Mr. Know-It-All walked by and said, "You know, I read a study that showed stretching doesn't prevent injuries when you work out."

"I hadn't heard that," I said, grunting as I reached for my toes.

When I got to the office, I logged on to the Internet and couldn't find the study that showed the uselessness of stretching; on the contrary, I found plenty of articles that talked about its value. I could add to them. Stretching just makes me feel better: My body is more relaxed; my back doesn't ache; I feel limber.

All day his comment irritated me; it was as though someone had told me, "Don't bother to pray. It doesn't do anything for you." I could point to countless studies that argued that point vociferously, but I don't pray because researchers tell me it's beneficial or effective. I pray because it's part of my life—my mind stretching to reach God, my heart bending toward Him. I can even do it while I'm stretching at the gym.

"Still at it?" Mr. Know-It-All asked me a couple days later at the gym.

"You should try it," I said with my arms over my head. "Stretching makes you feel good."

I reach out for You, Lord, as You reach out for me.

BLESSED TECHNOLOGY

*For the eyes of the Lord run to and
fro throughout the whole earth....*
—II CHRONICLES 16:9

Okay, I know that it's a real pain to be able to be reached anywhere by cell phone or computer, but you know, it can also be a real blessing.

The other night I was at the office, working a little too late on a Friday and feeling a little too sorry for myself but determined to get a job done. I was filling out an online form. Flummoxed by the technology, I couldn't figure out how to put an X in a box without the box disappearing. *This is what I get for not doing this when someone was around to help me.*

In a fury I sent an e-mail off to my colleague Nancy, attaching the form and asking her how I was supposed to do it. Nancy, of course—exquisitely organized Nancy—had left the office at a reasonable hour. I wouldn't hear from her until Monday morning.

If I said a prayer, it was one of exasperation. *God, why can't I figure this out?* All at once my computer made that friendly *brrrring* sound that it does when I have a message, and expecting another irritating piece of spam, I was delighted to see that it was Nancy—devoted, hardworking Nancy—responding from home. "Double-click on the box," she wrote, adding the crucial details.

It worked, of course. I had to be grateful for an office with people who check on their colleagues long after they should.

*Thank You, Lord, for the technology that links us
almost as fast as a prayer.*

A FORGIVING HEART

Be ye kind one to another, tenderhearted, forgiving one another,
even as God for Christ's sake hath forgiven you.
—EPHESIANS 4:32

I don't think I'm very good at forgiving," I told my friend Jim as we were having lunch at our favorite pizzeria. Not that I had anything specific in mind; just a vague feeling that I held on to grudges and kept track too closely of wrongs done to me.

"I can think of one place where you're good at forgiving."

"Where?"

"In your marriage."

"There's nothing much to forgive."

"There you have it." He took a large bite out of his slice of pizza and I chased an olive around my plate, finally stabbing it with my fork.

"Okay," I said. "I can remember a couple weeks ago being really irritated at Carol for not taking out the trash, but then as I was bagging it up, I remembered that she had been annoyed with me for not telling her that I was going to be late one night because of a meeting."

"Did she get angry at you?"

"Not for long."

"Did you get angry at her?"

"Not really... It all sort of evens out."

"That's because you forgive her."

I considered this insight for a moment and cut another slice of pizza. When I got home I'd have to inform Carol of this good news.

Give me a forgiving heart, Lord, as You have forgiven me.

LOVE THAT KEEPS US CLOSE

Many waters cannot quench love,
neither can the floods drown it....
—SONG OF SOLOMON 8:7

For six months this past year, our twenty-year-old son William was far away. I mean really far away. He did a semester of college in Melbourne, Australia. That's twenty-some hours of flying and fourteen time zones away! If he called us during the evening, it was late morning the next day for him! Yet he did call and e-mail us, the messages arriving instantly. I thought back to my college travel days when the only way to call home was to go to the post office of a foreign city, pay a hefty sum, and have an operator put you through. You had to holler to be heard—"My flight has been changed to Tuesday!"—across the Atlantic with waves of static rolling through the wires. But with William, we signed up for a service that wasn't expensive at all, and it was as if he was in the next room.

"What's that?" I would say, hearing a birdcall. *Some exotic Australian budgie?*

"I'm outside, Dad," he would say. "It's a beautiful day." Outside on a day that hadn't even gotten to us, talking on his cell phone.

But the best part was to hear the excitement in his voice about the koala bears in the eucalyptus trees, the kangaroo that kicked him, the nighttime sky in the outback, the game of footie (a sort of Australian football) he played with his classmates on a day that was spring for him, autumn for us. He wanted us to know that he was doing okay—better than okay—and I felt reassured that thousands of miles couldn't separate me from a love that's always there.

"Love you," I said, signing off.

"Love you too," he said.

Some amazing things aren't so newfangled after all.

Thank You, Lord, for the love—and technology—
that keeps my loved ones close.

SAVORING SPRING

For, Lo, the winter is past, the rain is over and gone.
—SONG OF SOLOMON 2:11

I spotted my bus turning the corner a couple of blocks away and I raced to catch it, darting through pedestrians, crossing the street against a flashing DON'T WALK sign, nearly running into a car. I could have gotten hit, I suppose, but all I was thinking was I have to get that bus! On Sunday afternoon buses don't come that often. And what would I do if I had to wait fifteen minutes for another one?

Despite my athletic prowess I still missed it. Now there was nothing to do but walk. In a huff I began my hike through the park, taking big strides on the path that wound under the pine trees.

It was early spring, the sky gray but the grass lime green, daffodils pushing up under the trees. A Little League team had gathered in a pine grove to practice. The wobbly tosses and swings proved it was early in the season. A kid raced past me on his bicycle, and a golden retriever scurried after a squirrel. I slowed my step. The smell of the damp earth, the sight of the buds, the sound of the whacked ball gave me a feeling of gladness. Winter was done. Spring was here. And to think, if I hadn't missed my bus, I would have missed it.

God, I love spring!

||||||||||||||||||||||||||||||||||||||||||||||||||||||||||||||||||||||||||||||||||||||||||||||||||||||

LIFE-TRANSFORMING FAITH

Ye shall seek me, and find me, when ye shall
search for me with all your heart.
—JEREMIAH 29:13

On the Friday after Easter, my colleague Ptolemy and I made a trip to the Abbey of Gethsemani outside Louisville, Kentucky. The place has been a spiritual landmark for me because of the writings of its most famous resident, Thomas Merton. A gifted poet and author, he entered the monastery in his twenties to devote himself to a life of prayer, teaching, and study. Here he wrote his autobiography, *The Seven Storey Mountain*, and it inspired me in my own spiritual search. But somehow a visit to the place where he lived was less than inspiring. Yes, we could see the sanctuary where he worshiped and the garden where he walked. In the bookstore we even spoke to one of the brothers who knew him. But I didn't feel as if I was meeting Merton.

"Go for a walk in the hills," a brother urged us, giving us a map. Ptolemy and I set off along the trail, trudging across fresh-mown pasture, winding through wooded hills, pausing at a sculpture garden, climbing a mountain where there was supposed to be a view of the abbey (hard to see through the trees). For a moment we got lost, and I worried that I'd brought Ptolemy on a wild-goose chase. He was good-natured, but I was fretting. It was getting late, and we needed to get back to Louisville. Then we came out of the woods onto a dirt lane leading to a meadow with a rusty old tractor, a red barn, and a rough-hewn cross.

That's when I met Merton...in that humble scene before me. I was reminded of how faith can transform the things of everyday life and how when you follow an unknown path—searching, trusting—God will lead you somewhere.

God, I know that in my seeking, however lost I feel,
You are there.

REMEMBERING THE FALLEN

The righteous shall be in everlasting remembrance.
—PSALM 112:6

Who's buried in Grant's Tomb? It's a bit of a one-line joke, but in all the years I've lived close to Grant's Tomb, and for all the times I've driven past it on its bluff overlooking the Hudson River, and even when the boys were in nursery school right next door, I'd never visited it. Neither had my wife. So on Memorial Day last year, after paying bills, doing some gardening, and feeling generally grateful to have a day to catch up, we set off on our expedition.

"Better get some gas first," Carol said, noticing the gauge. "Should we stop at the market on the way?"

By the time we got to Grant's Tomb and parked the car, it was 5:00 PM. "I wonder when it closes," I said, worried. We marched up the wide marble steps beneath the flags and bunting, and I pushed the door. Locked. I put my hands up to the glass and peered inside. Closes at 5:00 PM, said the sign.

All at once I felt foolish and selfish. Here was a chance to do what Memorial Day was set aside for, and we'd missed it through our own busyness. Yes, catch-up days are a blessing, but isn't it good to remember just what a holiday is for? I sank down on the steps, disappointed and irritated with myself.

Just then the door opened and a park ranger stepped out. "Would you like to come inside for a minute?" he asked.

Would we ever!

I can now tell you on full authority who's buried in Grant's Tomb: Gen. Ulysses S. Grant and his wife Julia. Next year I'll go back earlier, so I can tell you what else is to be found inside.

I shall not forget, Lord, the heroes of the past.

||||||||||||||||||||||||||||||||||||||||||||||||||||||||||||||||||||||||||||||||||||||||||||||||||

NEVER TIRED OF GIVING

"But when you do a kindness to someone, do it secretly...."
—MATTHEW 6:3 (TLB)

Let me introduce you to my colleague Colleen Hughes, the editor-in-chief of *Angels on Earth* magazine. In the years I've worked at Guideposts, I've always known her as one of those good office friends you can talk to about anything—

anything. She's sympathetic, thoughtful, generous, and she can make you laugh when it's just what you need.

One day this spring I was trying to think of something nice to do for her. (I couldn't begin to pay her back for all her kindnesses to me.) On Monday, on the way to work, I passed a flower shop with the most brilliant display of daffodils. *That's it!* I thought. I bought a couple of dozen, and early in the morning before anyone else got to work, I put them in a vase in her office. No note; just those buttery daffodils. Maybe, at last, I'd outgive her.

At 9:45 that morning, we gathered as usual in the conference room for Guideposts Prayer Fellowship. We were reviewing letters from readers and bringing up their prayer requests, when Colleen said, "I'd like to thank God for my flower angel today."

I've heard it said that a gift given in secret has extra value for the giver. I'll have to admit that being called an angel was more reward than I'd ever expected. Okay, so when Colleen reads this, the secret will be out. But in the meantime, I hope she's looking at all the angels in her life who are desperately trying to outgive her in ways they'll never reveal.

Let me never be weary, Lord, of giving.

QUICK TO FORGIVE

Forgive us our debts, as we forgive our debtors.
—MATTHEW 6:12

Somewhere I read that when you feel like blaming someone for some fault, you should look first to yourself to see how much of the fault might be yours. I suppose it's meant to be an exercise in forgiveness. Learning, as the Lord's Prayer puts it, to forgive others as I ask God to forgive me.

I didn't make much progress in this regard when we came back from our weekly trip to the supermarket, only to discover that the cashier had not put two items in our bag: the furniture polish and the stain stick for laundry. We had everything else, including the cookies I'd bought for the office, but no furniture polish or stain stick.

"Those are expensive things," I told my wife. "We shouldn't have paid for them if we didn't get them." I pulled out the long receipt and found that we'd been charged for both items. I waved it in fury.

"You can talk to them about it when we go back next week," Carol said, reasonably enough.

"But what proof do we have? Just a receipt. They'll never believe me." For the rest of the afternoon I fumed at the failure of people to do their jobs well. The sheer incompetence and laziness. The irresponsibility. Finally, I grudgingly recalled my spiritual goal about blaming. *Okay, Lord*, I said, *I forgive the cashier if You forgive me for getting so angry*. God and I left it at that.

Funny thing, though. The next day, when I lifted up the bag with the cookies for the office, it seemed heavier than usual. Guess what was inside?

When I'm about to blame someone, Lord,
let me start close to home first.

A MOTHER'S LOVE

Love never ends....
—I CORINTHIANS 13:8 (RSV)

Every year my mom opens up *Daily Guideposts* with anticipation—and dread. She enjoys reading the entries of all the contributors, but she makes a point of finding my devotionals first and telling me how much she likes them.

But dread, you ask? She's afraid I'm going to write about an incident when I was a kid and she got upset—a momentary lapse, let's say, in her parenting skills. So let me see if I can banish the dread once and for all.

Mom, I can't even begin to thank you for all the things you did right as a parent. You were patient, enthusiastic, fun, and full of praise. Thanks for teaching us how to play tennis, write thank-you notes, listen to music, and be a supportive friend. If we all have such good friends today, it's because we grew up watching you be such a good friend. If we all have good marriages, it's because we grew up seeing how you and Dad talked through your differences. You were a great Sunday school teacher, homeroom volunteer, art museum docent, and general organizer of a house with four children going in a thousand different directions.

I've asked Andrew, our editor, to slot this on your birthday, and when you see it I hope you'll know I mean every word. Happy birthday, Mom. You're the best!

Dear God, let me never grow tired of telling the people
I love how much they're loved.

CHILDREN ARE A BLESSING

In thee shall all families of the earth be blessed.
—GENESIS 12:3

I miss my older son William. I don't know why it should be worse this year than last when he first went off to college. I should have gotten used to it. But I ache at the sight of his empty bunk bed and the unnatural neatness of his desk, the faded posters on his walls and the stuffed animals on his bedspread. When do we start giving them away or getting rid of the Legos? Are we holding on to these things for him or for us?

Of course this is right. He should grow up. I'm proud that he's independent and manages to get good grades without having to be reminded to do his homework and finish his papers or be told that watching TV is not the way to study for a test. All that prodding was exhausting. Didn't I wish for the day when he could do it on his own? Shouldn't I be grateful he's not home?

Then the phone rings. "Hi, Dad," William says, nonchalant. No, nothing urgent to report. Just a few words about an economics class, his on-campus job, and the camping trip he might take over the weekend. I hang up, feeling better. There's something about loving your children that makes you worry about them and wonder about them more than they should ever have to know. I let William go—gladly, proudly—but a part of me is always thinking of him, my prayers spanning the distance between us. *Be with him, God. He's Yours.* Never more so than now.

What a blessing children are. Be with all of them, Lord.

SWEET SILENCE

Study to be quiet, and to do your own business....
—I THESSALONIANS 4:11

It was a summer day with temperatures in the upper nineties and no prospect of a cooling storm in sight. Our boys were off at camp, so it was just us two, Carol and me, dealing with the sweltering heat. I called a friend with a pool. "I won't be there," he said, "but feel free to go for a swim."

The sun was a fireball over the Hudson River as we drove out of the city. At seven o'clock that evening, the thermometer on the dashboard said ninety-eight degrees. The pool looked cool and inviting, surrounded by grass and trees. We dove in. Then Carol sat in a lawn chair and read through a stack of magazines while I stood at the water's edge with my book, a little like reading in the bathtub.

The trees trembled in a breeze, shrugging off the heat. The sun slid down the hill until it only illuminated the top branches, then disappeared. The tensions of the day fell from me like the water dripping from my elbows. The only sounds were the wind and the squirrels and the two of us turning our pages, like the companionable silence we shared as newlyweds before the boys were born, the quiet when nothing needs to be spoken because the most important words have been said.

After a while I could barely see the words on the page. "Ready to go?"

"Yes," Carol said, sighing. "That was perfect."

"It was, wasn't it?"

*Thank You, Lord, for the moments in my day
when silence speaks loudest.*

RESTLESS HEARTS

*Come unto me, all ye that labour and are heavy laden,
and I will give you rest.*
—MATTHEW 11:28

What do you want, Fred?" I asked our cat. "I wish you'd make up your mind." First he was meowing in the kitchen, then in the bedroom, and now at my feet. I was trying to do some work on the computer and there he was, butting against my leg. I reached down to scratch him between his ears. He seemed to enjoy it, purring contentedly, but the minute I stopped he sauntered back to the kitchen. "*Meow, meow,*" I heard him say.

"Okay, I give up. I'm coming," I said. I went into the kitchen. His water bowl was full, his food dish was half full, and my wife Carol had already brushed him once today. "What do you want?" I asked.

He looked up at me with his green eyes and said it again, "*Meow, meow.*"

I guess this is what it's like to be a cat, I thought. *Wanting things that you can't even articulate.* Then I paused. *No, maybe this is what it's like to be a human. Restless, impatient, needy. Sometimes I feel like wandering around the house and whining, wishing somebody would do something.*

I sat down on the floor. Fred nestled his head under the counter the way he often does and rolled over on his back so I could rub his stomach. "Do you know what St. Augustine once said about *his* Master?" I asked, running my hands through Fred's thick fur. "He said, 'Our hearts are restless until they rest in Thee.'"

He purred contentedly. I knew the feeling.

I come to You, Lord, looking for rest.

THE POWER OF THE WORD

The word of God is quick, and powerful, and sharper than any two-edged sword. . . .
—HEBREWS 4:12

My friend Arthur had several books on his hospital bedside table. A couple of contemporary novels, the day's newspaper, a magazine, and one small, tattered volume with a worn cover and pages that needed to be held together by a rubber band. Arthur's surgery had been a success and he was feeling better than he had in months. The doctor had only good news and promised that he'd be released soon.

"Do you have enough to keep you busy?" I asked.

"I think so." He gestured to the reading matter on his table.

"What about this?" I held up the slim volume that was falling apart. "Maybe you could afford to get a new copy," I joked.

"I like it just like it is. Take a look."

I slipped the rubber band off and was amazed. Every page had some marking on it. Red pencil underlining, blue ballpoint-pen check marks, words circled, comments in the margin. This book hadn't just been read; it had been a constant companion, a source of comfort and inspiration. I read a starred passage to myself, profound words by a writer who had thought deeply about faith and the human condition.

"I see why you like it," I said.

"I couldn't have gotten through the last twenty-five years without it," Arthur replied.

Leaving his hospital room, I was reminded of a quote I'd once seen on a church bulletin board: "The Bible that's falling apart usually belongs to a person who is not."

Dear God, may Your Word work through me so that I may become who You want me to be.

SHOWING UP

Praise him with the sound of the trumpet: praise him with the psaltery and harp.
—PSALM 150:3

Our son Tim has a rock band. Four sixteen-year-old boys who write their own songs, make recordings to post on their Web site, and practice whenever they can. This being New York City, where garages are hard to come by, they have to pool their babysitting money to rehearse in rented studio space. It's a little easier on our ears, but it means we didn't get a chance to hear them until they played their first gig at a club downtown with some other aspiring bands.

"What are we supposed to do?" I asked Carol. "Won't they be embarrassed if we show up?" I couldn't imagine anything less cool than a couple of proud parents in the back taking pictures. How would it look, this gray-haired intrusion?

"I'm not missing this for the world," Carol replied.

I felt pretty conspicuous in my blazer and buttoned-down shirt among the T-shirts and jeans. And I could have used a good pair of earplugs when the other bands played (it was loud, really loud). But when Tim's band performed, Carol and I hooted and hollered and clapped like the wildest of fans.

"You guys were awesome!" I told Tim. Their songs were clever—at least the lyrics I could understand—and their sound was great. And who knew that Tim could dance like Mick Jagger?

"Thanks for coming," he said in between a few high fives.

"Wouldn't have missed it for the world." That's what parents do. They show up...even in the most unlikely places.

I praise You, Lord, as I thank You for the gift of parenthood. Let my enthusiasm show!

||||||||||||||||||||||||||||||||||||||||||||||||||||||||||||||||||||||||||||||||||||

CONNECTING WITH NEIGHBORS

Thou shalt love thy neighbour as thyself....
—LEVITICUS 19:18

Someday our aging apartment building might get new plumbing that would allow owners to have their own washing machines, but I can only think of that prospect with a great sense of loss. I would miss our communal laundry room.

We have to walk down two flights of stairs, through the basement, then outside and down another flight of stairs to do our wash. Of course, it's not very convenient. Some days I've found myself dashing through a rainstorm to keep a bag of clean laundry from getting wet. In the summer the room can get steaming hot, and in the winter you need a sweater. And it's not always very tidy.

But it's the one place I know I can run into my neighbors and get a bit of news. I'll find out how Lauren's daughter is doing on her medical mission trip to Africa and how Roger's mother's health has been. Crystal will recommend a good book to read, and Margo will let me know how she's getting on with the book she's writing (only three more chapters to go!). Margaret and I, while folding, will compare notes on our churches and our children (guitar lessons going well, French homework not so good).

In the heart of this big and supposedly cold city of New York, going to the laundry room is like gathering around the old cracker barrel in a general store or seeing folks at the post office. It's what helps me follow the Golden Rule. Without it, I wouldn't know my neighbors so well or know how to love them. Washing, drying, sorting, folding—we get our wash-day chance to connect.

God bless my neighbors.

ADMITTING WHEN YOU'RE WRONG

Only by pride cometh contention....
—PROVERBS 13:10

I'm afraid I'm getting more stubborn with age. I used to be so flexible—or so it seems—but now I'm always so sure of myself. Not long ago at a dinner party with neighbors, I heard myself declare with absolute certainty to the woman next to me that a TV show we both watched was about the Korean War. "I don't think so," she said. "It's set during World War II." I disagreed—strenuously, dogmatically, with no room for argument. Then later we were talking about New York City geography.

"Rikers Island is in Sheepshead Bay," I declared.

"I don't think so," she said. "It's in the East River. You can see it from the Triborough Bridge."

"No, that's another island," I said. I should have admitted to some uncertainty, but I stuck to my guns. "Rikers is across town."

Only when I was home did I consult a map. You can imagine how foolish I felt to discover that my dinner companion was right. *Not much I can do about it now,* I thought. It would have been nice to apologize, but I couldn't even figure out how to bring it up.

Two days later I was on my morning jog through the park when I saw my neighbor, who was taking a brisk walk with a friend. *Now is the time,* I thought. *Just say it.* As we got close, I called out, "You were right about Rikers."

She smiled and waved. "You were right about Korea," she said.

I laughed and quickened my step. Perhaps admitting my mistakes is something else that can come with age. Half the time I might even be half right.

Dear God, let me be the first to admit I'm wrong.

||||||||||||||||||||||||||||||||||||||||||||||||||||||||||||||||||||||||||||||||||||||||||||||||||||||||||||||||||||||||||||||||||||

RED POPPIES

The righteous shall be in everlasting remembrance.
—PSALM 112:6

I was on a walk through the Yorkshire dales in England with two good friends. We'd come through a glorious countryside of rolling hills, stone walls, wildflowers, and enough sheep to film a biblical epic. We stopped for a water break beside a small stone farmhouse and admired the garden an older man was tending. He had roses, hydrangeas, vines of sweet peas, and, most spectacularly, dozens of red poppies. They reminded me of the crepe-paper ones my grandfather, a World War I vet, used to give us on Veterans Day.

"What a beautiful garden," I said to the farmer.

He nodded his head and muttered something incomprehensible—the local Yorkshire dialect could be pretty hard to decipher.

"I love the poppies," I added.

He said something else I didn't understand.

"Yes, yes." I nodded my head and walked on, trying to decipher his words. "Thanks for showing us your garden." Only a hundred yards later did I put it together, prompted by the memory of my grandfather's red crepe-paper poppies.

"Today is the ninetieth anniversary of the Battle of the Somme," the man had said in his thick Yorkshire accent. Red poppies had grown over too many soldiers' graves in Flanders fields. Red poppies commemorated one of the worst days of carnage in the history of warfare. Red poppies cared for by this farmer, probably because like millions of English families he had lost a relative in World War I.

He would never forget, and he didn't want others to forget, including three Americans hiking by his home on a beautiful summer's day.

Dear God, I pray for peace and an end to all wars.

|||||||||||||||||||||||||||||||||||||||||||||||||||||||||||||||||||||||||||||||||||||||||||||||||||

REFRESHING DIFFERENCES

Therefore shall a man leave his father and his mother, and shall cleave unto his wife: and they shall be one flesh.
—GENESIS 2:24

The light on the water is gold, the shadows under the bridge a deep purple, the sky a furious pink. "Look at the different colors under the bridge," I say to Carol. My wife stood for a moment beside me next to the Monet.

"Did you see the etching in the other room?" she asks.

"Which one?"

"The view of the Thames. It looks like a Japanese print."

"I'll check it out."

We wander through the exhibition, each of us pursuing our passions. She moves into a room of prints and drawings, and I stare a little longer at the colorful oil of London.

This is the way it often is in our marriage: Some things we do on our own, some things we do together. But even when we're off on our own, we're together.

There are things I want to tell her: "Big Ben looks flat and the arches of the bridge are very abstract. Is there a reason for that?" I'm curious about her reaction. After all, she's the art historian.

I wander through the museum, picking up more points for us to talk about. Does she still dislike Renoir? How about that little Degas sculpture? After twenty-three years of marriage, we know each other very well—and yet it seems as if we just met yesterday.

There she is in the last gallery, studying a diminutive drawing. "You know, the colors in that Monet were really amazing," she says.

"Do you still dislike Renoir?" I ask.

Lord, hear my prayer for the differences in life
that make each day new.

BLESSED IN GIVING

The Lord bless thee, and keep thee.
—NUMBERS 6:24

What would I do for Carol's fiftieth birthday? She made it clear that she didn't want a party, certainly not a surprise party (that was an agreement at our marriage—no surprise parties ever). "How about a small dinner with friends?" I asked. "No," she said, "I hate being the center of attention." Still, the milestone had to be marked. I wasn't going to let her get away with a Stouffer's frozen dinner and a movie video, which was all she claimed she wanted.

So I sent a letter to her friends, asking them for photos, poems, notes, cards, letters. "Carol doesn't want a party in person…but I'm hoping to give her a party in a book." I bought an album with a friend's advice, and the tributes poured in. For a few minutes at the end of every workday, I would pull out the marking pens and double-sided tape—who knew there were so many scrapbooking items?—and assemble the book, Carol's book. Photos of her in junior high, pictures of us with the boys, original songs, witty verse, fond reminiscences, and one haiku in Japanese. It made me grateful for all the years we've had together. The gift wasn't the album, it was the friendship and love she's given to me and to our kids and to all her friends and family. You could read it on every page.

I wrapped it up and took it home. "Happy birthday, sweetie," I said. "It's not a frozen dinner or a video, but it's what you deserve." She cried. She doesn't really like to cry, but I think she likes the book. She's said so many times. And every time I remind her that putting it together was a gift to me.

When I give, I always receive, thanks be to God.

BECOMING INDEPENDENT

I have chosen him to be my son, and I will be his father.
—I CHRONICLES 28:6

It's 5:40 AM, and I can hear William's alarm. He needs to take an early bus for his job as a counselor at a summer camp. When he was younger and had to wake up early, I would get up with him. I'd fix his breakfast, pack his lunch, and see him off. But he's eighteen now, and even if I wished to do those things, he prefers his independence. "You don't need to get up," he said the night before.

From my bed I am aware of his movements—the clank of his spoon against the cereal bowl, the front door opening as he picks up the paper, the water in the sink when he washes the dishes. His mom will be pleased that he remembered that, I think. I hear his duffel bag brush the floor. And I start wondering: *Does he have enough money? Did he remember to pack his retainer? Does he have any sunscreen?* Okay, he's a responsible kid, but I miss being needed. I fear that when that door finally slams shut, it's closing on me.

I need to trust that all that Carol and I have done as parents will hold him in good stead. Isn't that the whole point of parenting? If you do a good job, you put yourself out of a job.

I get up and tell him, "Have a good time at camp."

"Bye, Dad." He gives me a hug. Nice to be needed for that. Then the door slams shut, and I hear his footsteps scrambling down the sidewalk as he races to catch his bus.

Be with my child, Lord—Your child—as he steps into the world.

THIS GOOD EARTH

For the fruit of the Spirit is in all goodness and
righteousness and truth.
—EPHESIANS 5:9

What do I get from my garden? A few leaves of mint, some basil, a couple of cherry tomatoes, about five peony blossoms, one rosebud, and some parsley. An exceedingly modest summer crop, you may think. But my garden gives me an excuse to dig in the damp soil, to pull weeds with my bare hands, to clip a hedge and to smell the crushed grass, to shake off the petals from a flower, to feel the earth under my nails. To warm myself in the afternoon sun, to look for the rainbow in a spray of water, to catch a ladybug on my finger and let it fly away—not without making a wish. To know that there's always another season ahead in case this season feels too warm or too cold. The winter's frost will fade into spring's rains to be followed by summer heat and then autumn leaves. My garden takes me away from my checkbook and my unanswered e-mail. I'm reminded that there are things more permanent—and fleeting—in life, like dandelions, bees, and green blades of grass that you can hold between your fingers and blow on so that they sound like an oboe.

What does my garden give me? Patience, peace, perspective, and a chance to talk to my Maker. What better harvest?

I thank You, Lord, for this good earth and all its bounty.

HONORING THOSE FALLEN
IN BATTLE

These stones shall be for a memorial unto
the children of Israel for ever.
—JOSHUA 4:7

When publications run pictures of Memorial Day, they usually show cemeteries like Arlington with its thousands of pristine markers in unbroken waves or the American cemetery at Normandy with its countless crosses and stars of David. But the memory I have of the day is of quaint Mountain View Cemetery in the foothills of Pasadena, California, where my grandfather, a staunch member of the American Legion, made sure every veteran's grave was marked with a small American flag.

My grandfather, for reasons that were never clear to me, used to call us kids "you stick-in-the-muds." And I always thought of that expression on Memorial Day when we kids scattered through the cemetery in the day's waning light to collect the flags before sunset, digging them out of the mud. You could find them at the feet of the most ornate marble angel or next to a simple granite stone. Some of these graves had pretty rosebushes around them or fresh flowers in a vase nearby. Others were neglected and overgrown, as though no one had visited in years—not until our young feet scampered by. Most of the flags were for people I'd never known, some of whom, from the dates on their stones, died all too young. But all of them were, like my grandfather and father, veterans of war.

By sunset the flags were put away in boxes and bags in the back of Grampie's car, ready for next Memorial Day. We dashed home. But we all learned that remembering the dead wasn't passive. It was an action, something my grandfather organized year after year. And I suspect he asked us "stick-in-the-muds" to help him so that someday we would realize that thanks are owed to generation after generation, in graves fancy and plain, known and unknown, with more flags than fit in the back of a Buick. It's something you couldn't forget.

Lord, I give thanks for those who serve.

||||||||||||||||||||||||||||||||||||||||||||||||||||||||||||||||||||||||||||||||||||||||||||||||||||||||||

DEPENDABLE AND FULL
OF SURPRISES

O Lord, thou hast searched me and known me! Thou knowest when I sit down and when I rise up....
—PSALM 139:1–2 (RSV)

Father's Day and not a word from Timothy—not even a quick "Happy Father's Day!" at the breakfast table. It was not like him to forget Father's Day.

It made me nostalgic for Father's Days of the past when both boys were around. I could remember magical days at the ball field, cheering them on. I could recall picnic suppers in the park and handmade cards and clay creations. But not this year: William had a summer job in California, and in the afternoon we would be taking Timothy upstate to his job as a camp counselor. The day would be spent behind the wheel of a car. After the long drive, Carol and I would come home, eat dinner, and I'd watch Tim's and my favorite TV show all by myself.

That's all right, I told myself. *The boys are busy doing other things—as it should be at their ages.*

William called on the cell phone as we were driving back from camp. I was touched. But Timothy hadn't mentioned anything, even when I hugged him good-bye. The house seemed deathly quiet. I washed dishes, brushed my teeth, and went to watch TV. I was just about to plop myself down on the sofa when I noticed a bright turquoise envelope on my usual spot. "Papa," Timothy had written on the card inside, "I hope it's a good episode tonight, even without me there. Happy Father's Day!"

When someone loves you, they know you well…and know just where to find you.

Lord, let me be dependable—and full of surprises—
to those I love.

<hr>

LESSONS FROM JUDAS

Father, forgive them; for they know not what they do….
—LUKE 23:24

My Sunday school class of fifth and sixth graders was studying the Last Supper and Christ's betrayal. I wanted them to think about the disciple Judas and what his motives might have been. I wanted them to look more closely at what had happened those last few days of Christ's life. Maybe a bit of role playing would help.

"Here's the assignment," I said. "Each of you should imagine you're Judas. You're standing before God in heaven after the Crucifixion. What can you say for yourself? How can you justify the terrible thing you've done?"

"Who's going to play God?" one student asked.

"Me," I said, "at least for this exercise."

They came up with some interesting and rather sophisticated arguments. The Crucifixion wasn't really Judas' fault, said one boy. Judas only betrayed Christ at Jesus' urging, claimed another. After all, it was Jesus Who said, "Do what you must do." One girl went so far as to say that if Judas hadn't done what he'd done, there might not have been a Resurrection at all.

Still, none of the arguments moved me. Then one of the youngest boys in the class looked up a little sheepishly at me. "I'm really sorry," he said.

"What for?" I asked.

"That's what Judas should say. 'I'm really sorry. I had no idea what I was doing. Please forgive me. I would never have done it if I'd really understood Who He was.'"

I'm not God. I don't know how His conversation with Judas went. But as a Sunday school teacher I learned a lot that day. Arguments are compelling, but nothing is quite as powerful as asking for forgiveness.

I am sorry, Lord, and I repent for all the wrongs
I've committed.

SAVORING LIFE

I have not run in vain, neither laboured in vain.
—PHILIPPIANS 2:16

Dad found the perfect spot for himself this year on our beach vacation, at the end of the boardwalk in front of our two-week rental. He sat in his walker, his floppy hat on, a section of unread newspaper in his hands, and all those who passed by wished him good morning or stopped to chat. Some he knew; most were strangers, walkers and joggers doing the loop along the boardwalk. I went out to sit with him.

"They all like to touch the end," he said, speaking slowly, "either with their foot or their hand." It was as though they were in some race and had to touch the end of the old sun-bleached boardwalk for their mileage to count.

"What do you think about, sitting here?" I asked.

"Not much," he said. "There's too much to watch." There were the boats on the water, just visible over the sand; the waves rolling in; the swimmers treading out; and the runners and walkers marking their progress with the quick slap of a hand on the boardwalk wall.

I left Dad in his spot in the sun. He's lived a long, wonderful life and seemed especially glad to have his children and grandchildren close by for these two weeks. I watched him give the boardwalk a gentle tap as though he'd just completed a run. Then he stood up in his walker and came inside to join the family.

What a precious gift life is, Lord. Help me savor
every minute of it and every mile.

HAPPY FIFTIETH!

It is a good thing to give thanks unto the Lord....
—PSALM 92:1

For my fiftieth birthday I had an outrageous plan: a concert where I'd sing my favorite songs for my family and friends, and some of them would sing too. The highlight would be my fourteen-year-old son Timothy playing his guitar and singing The Beatles' "When I'm Sixty-Four." It would bring down the house. Only one downside—his older brother, seventeen-year-old William, wouldn't be there. He couldn't get away from school.

"I've got to study for finals, Dad," William explained.

"I know, I know," I said, thinking, *But I'm only going to be fifty once.*

I rented the hall, sent out the invitations, picked just the right hors d'oeuvres. Of course, I loved every minute of it: all those great people in one place; all that music that has meant so much to me over the years, one song after another. "And now," I announced, "from the next generation, I present the budding rock star, Timothy Hamlin!"

He strummed the opening chords, but his voice was hesitant. He seemed distracted. And then from the doorway I heard a second voice on the refrain. Timothy looked up and smiled. We all turned. There was William, singing in his strong baritone (and wearing my suit). Both their faces said, "Surprise, Dad!" It brought down the house. If I had ever doubted it for a moment, I knew then how blessed I am.

"That was the best song all night," I said. "You'd better do it again when I'm sixty-four!"

I rejoice, Lord, in all the blessings of life.

A PARENT'S PRAYERS

Let us take our journey, and let us go....
—GENESIS 33:12

Will gets into the driver's seat and I sit in the passenger seat, a change I'm not sure I can get used to.

"Okay, just pull away from the curb. Don't forget to look behind you. Check the rearview mirror. Yes, that's right. You're doing fine."

I want to be encouraging but, frankly, I'm scared out of my wits. He's taken driver's ed classes, but this is the first time we've done this together. He bites his lip. He's a little worried too.

"Do you see that stop sign ahead?"

"I see it, Dad."

"Good. Just let your passengers know you see it." I'm trying to put it in a way that won't sound alarmist. "You want to slow down, so they know you're going to stop in time." I feel my body jerk against the shoulder harness. Okay, it's a stop, just not a very smooth one.

"Which way should I go?"

"Let's turn right. There's a divided highway up there. It'll be good for practice." My mind thinks of all the challenges ahead. Highway driving, freeway driving, night driving. All the bad drivers on the road. The perils of the unexpected. I can find good reasons to be scared. But I look over at Will. He's always been very responsible. I trust him. Does he see the red light? Yes, and he's letting me know.

"How was that?"

"Nice stop." There must be a prayer for the parent of a driving teen. But then it's probably not much different from the prayers of a parent at any time.

||||||||||||||||||||||||||||||||||||||||||||||||||||||||||||||||||||||||||||||||||||||||||||||||||||||||

CHORES THAT PROMPT
THANKFULNESS

God setteth the solitary in families....
—PSALM 68:6

Socks, shorts, T-shirts, jeans, khakis.

A lot of T-shirts in Tim's pile. Twice as many as usual. I guess that means soccer season has started. All those practices after school mean one more dirty shirt a day. He loves soccer, but he's been worried about doing well on the team. The stakes are getting higher now that he's in high school. I want him to still enjoy playing. I pray that competitiveness doesn't get rid of the fun.

Will's socks. I can never match the socks right. Will's grown so tall and his feet are so long they look like flippers. He used to be able to wear my shoes, but he's outgrown my size. So why can't I tell his socks apart from mine? I have a pile of socks, and I'm just going to have to put them in pairs and hope they find the right drawers. He's almost an adult, but when I look at his socks I remember the tiny booties he once wore. God willing, he won't lose his childlike wonder as he grows into manhood.

Carol's bandannas. I think my wife uses them at the gym. Funny, I've never asked. I usually fold them into quarters so they can fit into a pocket like a handkerchief. They come in beautiful colors: turquoise, lemon, raspberry. And there's the one that has the map of nearby hiking trails on it. Reminds me of the spring day that we took one of those trails and hiked to the top of a mountain. We need to do that again.

Eventually everything's sorted and folded. Laundry is done. Sure, it's a chore, but when I do it, I'm reminded of what I love about the ones I love.

Lord, within this chore there's something to be thankful for.

NOT ALONE

Blessed are they which are called unto the marriage supper of the Lamb....
—REVELATION 19:9

Beryl was in church today. I was surprised. Pete, our deacon, told me the other day that she was confined to her apartment. She's ninety-nine years old and frail. When he took communion to her, he said she just looked at the bread in her lap, wondering what to do with it. How would she act during communion this morning? She stared around the church as if she were seeing it for the first time, which is certainly not the case.

I hated to think of her getting old. She and her daughter Carmen have been bulwarks in the congregation ever since we joined twenty-five years ago. They were always so warm, welcoming our newborns, monitoring the boys' growth, celebrating their baptisms and confirmations, rejoicing in the milestones of our life. For years they have been the church's unofficial greeters.

Communion came. Beryl rose unsteadily. She was in the second row. The whole congregation was focused on her.

Carmen took her hand, and they walked slowly to the front. Beryl paused, confused. Carmen didn't even have to look around. Another woman was right behind. She offered an elbow, and Beryl took it. All at once, Beryl seemed like a bride in a wedding, confident of where she was and what she was doing.

She took the bread and dipped it in the cup. She smiled. She returned ever so slowly to her seat.

"Send us out in the world in peace," we prayed, "and grant us strength and courage to love and serve You." I was glad I wasn't going out into that world alone. In Christ, I would be with Beryl and she would be with me.

We are never lost when we are with You, Lord.

<hr>

SOMEONE TO LOOK AFTER ME

Angels came and ministered unto him.
—MATTHEW 4:11

I was rushing to the airport on a business trip, afraid I'd miss my plane. You never know how long the line at security is going to be. I hurried through the terminal but was hungry. No food on this flight. I passed a stand. "Frozen yogurt," it advertised. The perfect thing. "One chocolate," I said. "In a cup."

I ate and walked, sat down to eat some more, got up to keep hurrying. To my relief, the line at security was short. I took my laptop out of its case, took the change out of my pocket, took off my belt. My shoes would be okay. But what was I going to do with my melting yogurt?

"Here," said the security guard, "let me take your yogurt." She put it in a plastic carton with the napkins so nothing would spill in the X-ray machine.

At the other end of security, I put on my belt, placed the laptop in its case, pocketed my change, picked up the yogurt, sticky in my hands, and turned to go.

"You forgot your napkins," the guard said.

I looked at her. She didn't look a whole lot like my wife Carol. The hair was the wrong color and the age wasn't right, but there was a certain similarity.

"You know, that's just the kind of thing my wife would remind me of," I said, picking up the napkins.

She smiled. "We wives are all alike."

"At least someone is looking out for me."

I'm glad to say that I arrived home without a spot of melted yogurt on my shirt, pants, or shoes. Business trips have their own angels, you know.

Dear Lord, thank You for those who remember what I forget.

<hr />

THE JOY OF BOOKS

Of making many books there is no end....
—ECCLESIASTES 12:12

B ooks furnish a room," my wife is fond of saying. A good thing, too, because our house threatens to be buried in books. We've got them furnishing every room: the hard covers in the dining room, the paperbacks in the TV room, the books that we intend to read on the floor by our beds, the books that we've read and intend to lend to friends on the cabinet. Every time we get a new shelf, it seems to fill up. First the books fill out rows, then get stacked in double rows, and then we start laying books horizontally on top. The only hope for us is our neighborhood's annual book fair. With pleasure, I deliver bags full of used books, all for a worthy cause.

For a couple of days our shelves look neater, our floors have more space on them, the house seems to have a little more air. Then comes the actual day of the book fair. Carol stops by, "just to see what's there." I drop in, "just to check on prices and maybe run into an old friend." Almost by accident I start looking down the row of books and spot many old friends...and new friends. *We don't have a copy of that*, I think. *Isn't that a nice edition? Haven't I always wanted to read that?* Surreptitiously, quietly, Carol and I gather books—bargains, I tell you, fabulous finds—and we take them home, sheepishly, apologetically. They start the journey from bedside table to shelf...and eventually to a bag for next year's book fair.

Open my eyes to the wisdom, Lord, in all I read.

MISGUIDED GENEROSITY

Who can understand his errors?
cleanse thou me from secret faults.
—PSALM 19:12

Our twenty-fifth reunion. My wife Carol and I were going back to the college we'd attended too many years ago to mention. Except we were mentioning it—advertising it, even. We were given shirts and jackets and belts emblazoned with the school colors and the number twenty-five. "No way will I recognize anybody!" I declared.

That first day I walked tremulously around campus, staring quickly at name tags before I ever said a name. It was a guessing game to find signs of the twenty-year-old self in the aged remains. Feeling more confident, I got better at it, greeting old friends boisterously.

In the afternoon, at the back of the college chapel, I saw Wade—I was sure it was Wade—with his wife and two kids. No name tag, but I could handle this one. "So good to see you!" I burst out, introducing myself to the wife and kids.

But after five minutes, the man wryly observed, "You seem to have mistaken me for some other handsome dude." If I'd been a chapel gargoyle, I would have turned to dust.

The rest of the reunion I kept telling friends, "I can't believe what a stupid thing I did! It was a guy here for his twentieth reunion. He wasn't even in our class!"

My pal Scott finally put the incident in perspective. "Rick, at least you erred on the side of friendliness."

Yes, and I've been given twenty-five years of forgiving friends.

Give me a generous spirit, Lord. Just don't let me
use it at the wrong time.

DIVISION OF LABOR

There are diversities of gifts, but the same Spirit.
—I CORINTHIANS 12:4

"Why do you always read the wedding announcements?" I asked my wife Carol, who is studying the wedding section in the *Sunday Times*.

"There might be someone here we know."

"Our friends all got married fifteen or twenty years ago. If it's anybody, it's going to be the children of friends."

"See?"

"I just don't know what's so important about the information you find there. Who somebody's parents are, who their grandparents are—why does that matter?"

"It interests me." It always amazes me that after eighteen years of marriage, with all the things we enjoy in common, we still have separate interests. Carol can't understand why I read the op-ed page. I can't imagine reading about weddings.

"Look," she says, delighted. "You know that young guy who lives downstairs? Here's his wedding announcement."

"We knew he was getting married. We met his fiancée. She's very nice. She already told you about her dress and bouquet and what the bridesmaids were going to wear."

"But look what it says about his family. This is an amazing coincidence. I worked for his grandmother the summer I was seventeen. Helped out at her summer home."

"How do you know it's the same woman?"

"It gives her husband's name and where she's from. Everything."

"Small world."

"Just think, we could have known the groom for years and I would never have known that about him. Not without reading the wedding announcements."

"Okay. From now on, tell me if you find something important in the wedding announcements."

"And you tell me what's on the op-ed page." It's a division of labor, as good a reason as any for God to bring two people together. The whole is always greater than the sum of the parts.

Help me grow, Lord, as I learn how little I know.

|||||||||||||||||||||||||||||||||||||||||||||||||||||||||||||||||||||||||||||||||||||||||||||||||||||||||||||||||||

THIRTY DAYS OF PRAYER

Pray one for another, that ye may be healed....
—JAMES 5:16

L og on.
PASSWORD.

"Dadshealth," I typed. Dad had had a bad cold lately. Maybe the symptoms indicated something more serious. I'd been worried about him. That's why I'd made "Dadshealth" my password—a reminder to pray for him.

YOU HAVE TWELVE DAYS TO CHANGE YOUR PASSWORD. DO YOU WANT TO CHANGE IT NOW? my computer asked me.

"No," I told the computer. Dad wasn't out of the woods yet. He was doing better though. The doctor had run some tests. We'd find out if it was serious.

Twelve days. That must have meant I'd been praying for him for eighteen days, because my password has to be changed

~ 58 ~

every thirty days. Another prayer today, then I punched the Enter key. Time for work.

Three-thirty in the afternoon. The work had been so involving I hadn't really thought about Dad. E-mails, phone calls, snail mail, memos, manuscripts—they came at a rate that made me think I'd never catch up. One more call. I answered it.

"Hi!" It was Dad. "Just wanted you to know that the tests all came out fine. The doctor says in another week or two I'll be well." Two weeks. That's almost twelve days.

"Good, Dad. I'll keep you in my prayers." I'd keep him in my password too.

Some years ago in Guideposts there was an article that claimed if you prayed for something for thirty days you'd get results. Thirty days. And you know what? In thirty days I've always found that the urgency that led me to the prayer in the first place has diminished.

An answer in thirty days? Well, yes, there is an answer. Try it. Just for thirty days.

Starting today and for the next twenty-nine days, Lord,
   I will pray for _____.
                        (INSERT NAME)

||||||||||||||||||||||||||||||||||||||||||||||||||||||||||||||||||||||||||||||||||||||||||||||||

WORSHIPFUL SILENCE

The Lord is in his holy temple: let all the earth
keep silence before him.
—HABAKKUK 2:20

There was simply too much noise. Sunday morning I was teaching, as usual, my rambunctious class of third, fourth, and fifth graders. We had already gone over the lesson about Paul on the road to Damascus, acting out his blinded-by-the-light conversion. At one point I had a roomful of kids lying on the ground as one of them read Christ's words, "Why do you persecute me, Paul?" But then things started to get rowdy.

As the noise level increased, I raised my voice in exasperation. "Okay, I have a special assignment for today. I want you to do two things. First, make as much noise as you can for two minutes. Then be absolutely silent for two minutes. I dare you to do both."

Gleefully they met my challenge. First they made an unholy racket, yelling, shouting, and clapping. (Fortunately, our classroom is in a distant corner of the parish house.) The odd thing was, they couldn't keep it up at top volume for very long. After a minute they began to look expectantly at me. "Can we stop now?" I shook my head. Finally, after two minutes, I announced, "Silence."

Eyes closed, heads bowed, hands came down, and they were blissfully quiet. No snickering, no kicking, no guffawing. Two minutes of such silence I think I could hear their hearts beat. When time was up I asked, "Which felt more natural? Which was more comfortable? Which was closer to God?"

Take two minutes and find out for yourself.

God, I worship You not only with joyous noise
but also with blessed silence.

A SACRED CIRCLE

A friend loveth at all times....
—PROVERBS 17:17

For several days I'd been mulling over the question I'd been asked: "How do you know when to take someone off your prayer list?" I looked at the slip of paper in my Bible and the names that had been on it for years. I had tried to be diligent, crossing off a name when a need had been answered—when a hospitalized friend was out of the danger zone or when a marriage was no longer in trouble. But I had to admit, there were people on that list whom I hadn't prayed for in years. Why didn't I take them off? Why did I find that as hard as dropping someone from a Christmas card list?

Then one afternoon I was flipping through my Rolodex and I came across the name of a friend I hadn't seen in months. Once, in fact, during a trying time when he was searching for a new job, he'd been at the top of my prayer list. Since then, he'd found an ideal position. But how was he doing now? How was his career going? After several calls, I reached him at his new office. When we met for lunch a week later I got a complete update—and one new good reason to remember him in my prayers. "You're on my list," I said in parting.

On my way back to the office I reflected on my habits of intercessory prayer. People come and go in my intercessions, as their needs change, but when I'm current with the lives of my friends and family, I find it very easy and very natural to pray for them. My prayer list should be flexible, like a sacred circle. I update it as I hear from people. Then I pray. By praying, I keep in touch—and by keeping in touch, my prayer life improves.

Lord, I ask You to be with _____,
(INSERT NAME)
who is in great need today.

BROTHER ON THE GO

He causeth the vapours to ascend from the ends of the earth;
he maketh lightnings for the rain; he bringeth the wind....
—PSALM 135:7

As a boy, my older brother Howard was always hard to pin down. He could be building a fort in the backyard, riding his minibike down the block, racing his go-cart at the school lot, or digging a tunnel in the field next door. That he managed to come home in one piece was no doubt a tribute to providence.

Age and marriage have mellowed most of us. Not Howard. He still is always on the go, almost impossible to keep track of. A competitive sailor, he participates in races all over the world. And when he's not sailing, he could easily be skiing in Canada or surfing in the South Pacific or at home in California. "Where's Howard?" is a frequent familial inquiry. My mom once told me that she never could go to bed at night until she pictured where all of us were—then prayed. Howard must be a continual challenge to her imaginative skills.

Then last year he was on the crew of Steve Fossett's sailboat *Play Station Two*, attempting a new record for circling the British Isles. Suddenly we all knew exactly where Howard was. We could log on to the Internet and watch his progress. The Web site was so precise it showed the boat every step of the four-day journey, with constant updates on the weather. We watched during the squalls, the jibes, the torturous hours when they were becalmed in the Irish Sea. And the thrilling finale when they picked up thirty-knot winds that brought them into Southampton with a new world's record.

"It must be our prayers that brought you around," I e-mailed him.

"It had to be something," he e-mailed back.

Dear Lord, thanks for the technology that helps me keep in touch with those far and near.

THE HARDEST PRAYER OF ALL

Love your enemies, bless them that curse you … and pray for them which despitefully use you …
—MATTHEW 5:44

Odd what can get me riled up. For months I seethed with rage at the mere mention of a certain political figure. I flew into a fit at his remarks in the newspaper. I bored my friends to tears with my tirades against his policies. I could bring any dinner party to a halt with my views.

So one Monday morning when I had to change my password on the computer, I was surprised to find myself thinking of this person. You see, my password is always the name of someone I need to pray for that month. But … pray for my archenemy? Pray for my political nemesis?

I winced and entered the name. And for the next month I prayed for him. I still got riled up at the mention of his name—

still argued with his comments in the newspapers—but as the month wore on, I started thinking about why he believed in what he believed. And how he'd come to those decisions. I won't go so far as to tell you that I'll vote for him. But at least I understand.

Odd what prayer will do for you. It can even turn an enemy into a friend.

Dear God, give me words for the hardest prayer of all:
to learn to love.

<hr/>

FRED THE CAT

Every creature of God is good....
—I TIMOTHY 4:4

I've always thought the world was divided into cat people and dog people. Carol was one of the former, and I was definitely one of the latter. I loved big dogs with wagging tails, and she loved furry, purring kittens—a standoff. The best solution for twenty years of marriage was that we owned neither dog nor cat.

Then our friend Mary Alice rescued an eight-month-old kitten on a subway platform in Harlem. "He's very pretty," she told Carol. "Long, fluffy, gray hair with neat white paws." The problem was that Mary Alice couldn't keep him. Would we be interested?

"No," I said. "I don't want some beast meowing around the house, sitting in my lap when I'm trying to work, begging to be petted."

"Mary Alice asked if we could just take him for a couple nights until she finds a home for him."

"I suppose so."

Can you guess the rest of the story? The cat—christened Fred because he was found on Frederick Douglass Boulevard—has become my great pal. Delighted, I wake up to Fred licking my ear. I eat breakfast with him at my feet. When I come home at night, he's the first one to greet me. "Meow, meow," he says. *Play with me!* And I do.

The scariest thought is if I had clung to my preconceived notions, I would never have known the pleasures of working at the computer with a purring cat in my lap. All I needed was a little nudge.

Now I wonder, though, what would Carol—and Fred— think of adding a mutt to our ménage?

Open my eyes, Lord, to the beauty of all Your creatures.

||||||||||||||||||||||||||||||||||||||||||||||||||||||||||||||||||||||||||||||||||||||||||||||||||||||||||

THE BETTER INVITATION CLUB

I have shewed you kindness, that ye will also shew kindness....
—JOSHUA 2:12

Van—Van Varner to those of you who aren't veteran *Daily Guideposts* readers—always says that he's not a member of the Better Invitation Club. It's a moral principle, as I've come to understand, or putting the Golden Rule into practice: If someone invites you to do something, you don't ditch them because a better invitation happened to come your way.

I thought of this ten years ago when we received an invitation to Van's seventieth birthday party. What a bash it would be! Good friends gathered together to reminisce over his seven decades and cheer him on for more. "But we can't go," my wife said. We'd already promised to join several old friends at the beach that weekend. I was tempted to see if the beach trip could be rearranged, then remembered how hard it had been to schedule in the first place. Well, if anyone would understand, it would have to be Van. "Next time," I told him. "Next time," he agreed and added another of his favorite phrases: "God willing."

So for almost ten years I saved the date: June 6, 2003. This time when the invitation arrived, the decks were clear. No conflicts. Even if the president of the United States had invited us to dine, I would have refused, saying, "We're not members of the Better Invitation Club." It's a moral principle, you know, and it seems to ensure a long happy life with the very best of friends. Not to mention invitations that you'd never want to turn down…God willing.

*Courtesy is kindness, Lord. Let me do as
I would have done unto me.*

||||||||||||||||||||||||||||||||||||||||||||||||||||||||||||||||||||||||||||||||||||||||||||||||||||||||||||||||||

MOM FOR A DAY

*Adam called his wife's name Eve; because she was
the mother of all living.*
—GENESIS 3:20

What to get my wife Carol for Mother's Day? There was a book she wanted and a CD. The boys had made cards…but it'd be nice to show her how much I appreciate all that she does: the cooking, the carpooling, the shopping, supervising the homework, arranging the doctors' appointments and music lessons.

"Take the day off," I said. "Enjoy yourself."

"Really?"

"Sure. We'll be fine."

That Sunday Timothy and I did the week's grocery shopping and got dinner ready, and I supervised his homework. In the late afternoon I took him to his soccer game and brought him home. But just as we pulled into the driveway, he frowned. "Dad, I think I left my sweatshirt back at the field."

"Are you sure?"

He nodded gravely.

An hour later we returned home after searching the field in the waning light.

"Where have you been?" Carol asked.

"A little detour," I said. How to explain that the dirty sweatshirt on her son's back was part of her present? "I guess I found out how complicated your days really are," I said. "Happy Mother's Day!"

God, help me remember how much work it takes to be a mother.

||||||||||||||||||||||||||||||||||||||||||||||||||||||||||||||||||||||||||||||||

TRUSTING GOD WITH MY KIDS

"Be strong and of good courage; be not frightened, neither be dismayed; for the Lord your God is with you wherever you go."
—JOSHUA 1:9 (RSV)

When choosing a boarding school, our older son Will declared that he didn't want to go to a church-affiliated school. No mandatory chapel. No Bible classes. "There are some excellent schools in our denomination," I pointed out.

"He's looking to do things his way," Carol explained. After all, for fourteen years he'd gone to church almost every Sunday morning with us. Now he wanted to spread his wings. "He's pretty good at making decisions on his own," she went on. "We need to trust his judgment in this."

So off he went to New Hampshire to an excellent school. For that first year we got e-mails and phone calls about his friends, his classes, his extracurricular activities. But no reports on any Sunday worship services. On Parents Weekend we went to chapel on our own. He slept in.

But then a curious thing happened. In his sophomore year he announced that he'd found a local church with services on Wednesday at midday—"so I won't have to get up early." He volunteered for community service. He took cookies to their Maundy Thursday evening dinner. And one Sunday he called and said, "I heard the best sermon this morning. The Bible verse was just what I needed to hear: 'Be strong and of good courage; be not frightened, neither be dismayed; for the Lord your God is with you wherever you go.'"

I don't know what decided Will to reacquaint himself with church—whether it was a tough Latin class or the memory of a habit from home. But I'm glad he's sorting things out on his own. In the meanwhile, it's not just Will I'm learning to trust.

God, we give You our children. They have been Yours all along.

DRIVEN TO MY KNEES

Incline thine ear, O Lord, and hear....
—ISAIAH 37:17

Carol and I weren't in New York City the day the World Trade Center was attacked by terrorists. We were in New Hampshire, delivering our son William to his boarding school. Instead of seeing those horrible events from my office window, I watched them on TV. Like everyone else tuned in to the news, I was horrified. The rest of the day, in this placid New England setting, I could only think about what was happening back home in New York. Was anyone we knew trapped inside those buildings? Was everyone at our office okay? Our younger son Tim was in school in New York that day. I was sure he would get home safely with friends. But how would he feel? The lines were clogged, and we couldn't reach him or anyone by phone.

During an orientation meeting I could barely concentrate. "I have to go outside," I told my wife, and slipped out. I paced on the sidewalk and did the only thing I could think of: I prayed. *Jesus Christ, have mercy on us. Make haste to help us. Rescue us and save us. Let Thy will be done in our lives.* I must have repeated that prayer a hundred times before I felt some peace. No answers, just a measure of peace. I went back inside and arrived in time to hear the school minister leading the parents in prayer. More of what I desperately needed.

Driving home that afternoon, Carol and I listened to whatever radio stations we could pick up. Reporters gave updates, statesmen made comments. Someone invoked the name of Abraham Lincoln, president the last time there was warfare on American soil. Things must have seemed as bewildering to him back then as they were to me for the moment. How did Lincoln find hope in the midst of that terrible conflict? Where did he turn for guidance? Then I recalled something he once said: "I have been driven many times upon my knees by the overwhelming conviction that I had nowhere else to go." The only reasonable thing to do.

> *Let me never forget to turn to You, God, when*
> *there is nowhere else to turn.*

||||||||||||||||||||||||||||||||||||||||||||||||||||||||||||||||||||||||||||||||||||||||||||||||||||||||||||||||

WHEN WORDS WON'T SUFFICE

God shall wipe away all tears from their eyes.
—REVELATION 7:17

What could I say? I'd already tried, and my words sounded hollow. A neighbor, a dear friend, had lost his wife to cancer, leaving behind their sixteen-year-old son. I could remember long summer afternoons sitting in the neighborhood playground with her, watching our sons build sandbox castles. We'd done birthday parties together and sleepovers and picnics where the adults tried to stay as far away from the swimming pool as possible, avoiding getting splashed by the Marco Polo players.

"Could you just watch the kids for a minute?" I would say to her.

And she would say the same to us. We'd thrown balls, gone on bike rides, and seen our boys grow so old they pretended they didn't need us any longer. We weren't fooled. Her death was a terrible loss. What could I possibly say to her husband to relieve his grief?

I wrote what I could in a card. I said a few words to him at the service. But all of it felt so small. Then one night I was rushing back from the car, my arms filled with the dry cleaning. I passed him in the dark, at first not even realizing who it was. I stopped, turned around, called to him, draped my cleaned shirts on a bush, and the two of us hugged.

God be with you. Words wouldn't suffice. Someday they'd come. But for now, as long as he knew that he was not alone. Not at all.

> *Give me actions when words don't come, God, and*
> *words to match my actions.*

IIIIIIIIIIIIIIIIIIIIIIIIIIIIIIIIIIIIIIIIIIIIIIIIIIIIIIIIIIIIIIIIIIIIIIIIIIIIIIIIIIIIIIIIIIIIIIIIIIIII

THE BLESSING OF NEIGHBORS

> *Better is a neighbor that is near than a brother far off.*
> —PROVERBS 27:10

You might be surprised to hear that I live in a small village on the island of Manhattan in New York. This particular village—one of many in New York City—is a 324-unit cooperative apartment complex housing about five hundred people. We're held together by proprietary leases and corporate bylaws; we pay fees for the upkeep of the grounds and buildings; and we have a board of directors and endless meetings to decide things like where a new laundry room should go. But we're also bonded by other things.

For instance, there are the "Who's Got Soup" volunteers who provide hot meals for anyone who can't get out, and the weekly shuttle bus that takes people to the big discount market. There are bingo nights and Fourth of July parties and visits from Santa for the kids. But there are also all the people whom we know by their habits: the Juilliard cellist we hear through open windows on warm spring nights; the centenarian who requested "long-life bulbs" from the maintenance man—we all chuckled at that story; the building superintendent who trades football scores with the boys.

One day not long ago, I couldn't get one of our elderly neighbors on the phone. She hadn't been feeling well, and I was worried. I knocked on her door. I called through the mail slot. Finally, I asked the super, who has a set of keys to the apartment, if we could go check on her. He readily agreed. This story has a happy ending: My neighbor was visiting a relative. But what I remember most about that day were the super's words when we discovered the apartment was empty: "I was praying for her. I was praying for her the whole time." That's one of the things that keeps a village together.

Keep my neighbors safe in Your care, Lord.

—————————————————————————————

PATIENCE FOR PARENTING

The patient in spirit is better than the proud in spirit.
—ECCLESIASTES 7:8

I don't have any good ideas for a haiku!" my son Timothy wailed.

"Sure, you do," I said, mustering all the patience I could gather. "Look out the window. Write about what you see. Five syllables: 'The sky is a whale…'"

"That's dumb, Dad."

"It's a start. Get working and something will come up."

The doorbell rang.

I opened the door. "Baby Sam," Timothy said. Our neighbors were dropping off their seven-week-old infant for us to baby-sit. They came in with bottles, diapers, blankets, a Baby Bjorn infant carrier. It was their first time out together without the baby.

"He'll be fine," I said, lifting him out of his mother's arms. He was so soft and cuddly. All we'd have to do was hold him for an hour or two. *It'll be a lot easier than helping a twelve-year-old with his homework*, I thought.

"Bye-bye," we said to Sam's parents.

"You do your haiku," I told Timothy. I showed Sam around the house, his blue eyes catching the light, his little fingers grabbing hold of mine. And then he began to cry. I tried the football hold, then the Baby Bjorn. Sam continued to cry.

"I'll bet you need a bottle," I said, warming one up in the sink. "That's it, you're hungry." He guzzled for a few minutes. I burped him. He cried some more.

"He's tired," I explained to Timothy. I put him back in the Baby Bjorn and we walked around the house. Finally, he went to sleep—and woke up fifteen minutes later.

"His diaper needs changing," I said, and changed it. He cried.

He stopped just the moment his parents returned. "Thank you so much," his mother said. "We needed a break."

"All parents do," I agreed before I went back to supervising the haiku.

"Here's one," I said to Timothy. "'That's what I got through./ Now I know I can get through/What I'm going through.'"

Timothy scrunched his nose at me. "I can do better than that."

"I believe you can."

~ 73 ~

Give me the patience, Lord, to be a good parent,
for every age brings its challenges.

GOOD STEWARDSHIP

It is required in stewards, that a man be found faithful.
—1 CORINTHIANS 4:2

I had been asked to speak on stewardship at a friend's church. "Sure," I said, flattered. But as the date approached, I was wracking my brain for good examples. Of course, I could find the predictable ones: people who volunteer at soup kitchens, homeless shelters, Sunday schools. But could I think of something less predictable? For instance, how about stewardship at work?

Then I recalled Nancy Schraffenberger. Nancy was a senior editor and I a lowly assistant editor when I first came to Guideposts. After six months, I was asked to take over several of the departments she had edited. She explained what the job would entail, supervised me through a couple of revisions of stories, then handed me the files. At once I was in charge of an intimidating inventory of manuscripts and clippings. As I looked at that pile, I wondered how I would manage. But delving into the inventory over the next few months, I discovered more signs of Nancy. Comments that she'd made on manuscripts, correspondence with authors, edited pieces that were so good they were ready to put into type. None of it was to show off to our boss. Instead, it was her quiet way of supporting me until I came up to speed in the job.

"Good stewardship is making the most of the resources you're given so that when you pass them on they're in even better shape." That was how I put it in my speech. But you'll have to ask the person who later took over those files what kind of steward I was. Would that she could say I'd done my job as well as Nancy Schraffenberger did hers.

Help me make the most of all that You've given me, Lord.

MAKING TIME FOR FRIENDS

We took sweet counsel together....
—PSALM 55:14

B astille day is coming up," David's message says. I call him back and leave a message on his phone: "Shall we eat at the same place?" He leaves a new message: "See you there!"

Voice mail is our easiest means of communication. Both of us are busy; it's been months since I last saw David, and he's one of my oldest pals. Good thing that Bastille Day is coming up.

There he is at the unpretentious French place around the corner from the office. We greet each other with a hug, sit down, and soon we're off, catching up on six months of news: His son was in a bike accident but is doing just fine; his wife is changing the focus of her career; his daughter is having a great time at summer camp. Here we are living in the same city, and I hadn't heard any of it. Good thing we've gotten together.

We make our way through the pâté and the poulet and the pommes frites, when I remember the tricolor dessert that's a necessity for the holiday: bleu, blanc et rouge, a blueberry, strawberry, and cream tart. Better save some room for that!

Neither of us is French, nor are we particularly Francophile. I guess we'd go in for Liberty, Equality, and Fraternity, those French virtues of the day. The point is, once, we got together on Bastille Day and we've made it our red-letter day ever since. It's when we put friendship on the calendar. Otherwise it gets lost in the shuffle.

"Happy Bastille Day!" we say to each other at the end of the meal. And polish off that tricolor tart.

Lord, I will never be too busy for a friend.

MAKING A DIFFERENCE

Whatsoever thy hand findeth to do, do it with thy might....
—ECCLESIASTES 9:10

My wife Carol says I've become a real crank about litter. It drives me nuts. I don't like to see it along the highway, in the streets, at the park where my son plays Little League games, hiking in the woods. It's one of society's ills, I complain. Nobody feels responsible anymore. "Well then, do something about it," Carol said one day.

Chastened, I brought a pair of old gardening gloves and some black plastic garbage bags to my son's baseball game the next week. "What are those for?" he asked.

"A little project," I said. But, boy, am I ever going to feel dumb collecting empty soda cans out beyond left field when all the other parents are watching their kids warm up. "Have a good practice."

As conspicuous as a clown at a birthday party, I made my way across the grass, kneeling over every gum wrapper, Popsicle stick, and juice carton. By the time I reached those soda cans, my black bag was half full. Virtue might be its own reward, but I was still feeling foolish. I stood up to empty a bottle of orange soda—at least the guy could have finished his drink—when I noticed a pair of dads heading my way. "Need some help?" one of them hollered.

"Sure." I gave them two bags, and we continued to work, talking about our kids, their games, the park. When we were finished, I had two new friends and a pristine field.

"You know," I said to my wife a little smugly, "society's ills can be solved when people get together to do something about them."

"Sure beats complaining," she replied.

Lord, don't let my pride prevent me from making a difference.

A QUEEN'S PRIORITIES

Henceforth there is laid up for me a crown of righteousness, which the lord, the righteous judge, shall give me at that day....
—II TIMOTHY 4:8

The alarm went off well before the usual hour. I glanced first at my bedside clock. Five o'clock. Why so early? I turned to see my wife getting out of bed. "Why are you getting up so early?" I whispered, as though I might wake her.

"I have to watch TV," Carol whispered back.

"Oh." I rolled over and attempted to sleep. But light was coming from the kitchen, the coffee was dripping, and then came a low murmur from the TV down the hall. Singing, too. I dozed for a few minutes and returned to the sound. A sonorous British voice, the clip-clop of horses, tolling of bells, an organ echoing down a long nave, singing again. This for the death of a queen.

Giving up on sleep, I went into the TV room to find my wife on the couch with a cup of coffee, a box of tissues, and an open hymnal. "Crown Him with Many Crowns," they were singing on TV. "That's an odd thing to sing at a funeral," I said.

"Not at all," Carol said. "That was her special request."

"You'd think she'd had enough of crowns." She'd worn one for decades.

"That's what is so sweet," Carol said, grabbing a tissue. "She wanted to show that she had her priorities straight."

I decided then not to tease Carol over her royal-watching and incurable Anglophilia. There was something right about the Queen Mum's parting gesture and the thought that millions were partaking of it, like my wife, with their own cups of coffee in front of their own TVs. I sat down and hummed along, joining the global congregation.

Lord, may a life of service be my own crown.

||||||||||||||||||||||||||||||||||||||||||||||||||||||||||||||||||||||||||||||||||||||||||||||||||||||||

CHEERFUL GIVING

Give, and it shall be given unto you....
—LUKE 6:38

Two boxes of fig Newtons and one package of Oreos. I had them in a shopping bag on my lap as I sat on the subway heading to work. They were part of my stash to add to the communal cookie drawer at the office. Everyone gives some and everyone takes. It always seems to work out. It was my turn to donate.

"Could you give me twenty-five cents so I can get something to eat?" an agitated voice said. A poor wretch was coming down the length of the car shaking a tin cup. With my eyes closed, I was attempting to concentrate on the lesson I'd just read from the Bible—using this morning commute time for a bit of contemplation—but I looked up. There he was in tattered dungarees, his hair unkempt and his dirty toes peeking out of holes in his boots. I could smell him, too.

My eyes closed again, I could envision the words printed on a public-service notice across from me: "Don't give to beggars on the subway. Give to charities that will help them." I knew the arguments well. Most of these poor souls are suffering from mental illnesses. Many of them will spend whatever you donate on drugs or drink. They need more than a handout. But hadn't the passage in the Bible urged me to give as God gives to me?

At least he could eat the Fig Newtons, I reasoned. I opened up a package and gave him one cellophane wrapper full. The office would understand. He thanked me, and I closed my eyes once again. This time I found it much easier to concentrate on the Bible passage.

"Somebody ate half this box of Fig Newtons," a colleague at the office pointed out.

"It went to a worthy cause," I said.

Lord, let me give cheerfully, unhesitatingly,
all that I've been given.

═══

MARK OF THE HEALER

With his stripes we are healed.
—ISAIAH 53:5

Good morning, Erin," I said first thing that February day. She was working at the reception desk and I was rushing to my office. "How are you?" I asked rather automatically. I had a thousand things on my mind.

"Fine," she replied. Something in her voice made me stop. "What's wrong?"

"I was in a car accident last night." Her lip quivered, and I noticed the bump on her forehead.

"Are you all right?"

"I thought I was. I wasn't hurt much. I'm lucky. The other driver ran a red light. But now I'm feeling kind of shaky."

"If you need to go home..."

"No. I'd rather be here. I need to be around people." Others arrived, and we listened to her, somebody got her some coffee, and the volunteer EMT in the office inspected her forehead more closely. Reassured that Erin would be okay, we went to our desks, but we were all left wondering what more we could do. An ice pack? Aspirin? Could I get her some lunch?

At midday she was gone. "She went out," someone told me. *Good,* I thought. She'll get some fresh air, some lunch. When I returned from my lunch, she was back at the front desk and looked a lot more relaxed. "I'm feeling much better," she said.

But your forehead, I was about to say. There was a dark smudge over the bump. Had the bruise gotten worse? Then I remembered the day: Ash Wednesday, the start of Lent. The smudge was a bit of ash in the shape of a cross. She was wearing the mark of the Healer.

"You found the right place to go at lunch," I said.

"It helped a lot," she added.

In faith, Lord, I turn to You for healing.

THE PASSING TIME

My times are in thy hand....
—PSALM 31:15

Twenty-six years ago, when still a student, I spent an unexpected tax refund on a really good watch. For twenty-six years I never took off that watch. Waterproof, shockproof, shatterproof, it went with me everywhere. With it, I could keep a constant check on the time: sneaking a glance at my watch during meetings at work; stretching my arm surreptitiously at church just to clock the sermon; holding the luminous dial up to my eye at the movies to see if a film was finishing up.

Then, on a sultry summer day at the beach, I took a wave badly in rough surf and tumbled headfirst into the sand. The watch—this reliable companion—slipped off my wrist as I was tossed in the turbulence. I swam after it, but another wave was on top of me. I stood up in the water, trying to catch the watch in the sand with my toe. *It's got to be here someplace,* I thought. I marked the spot, thinking that when the tide went out I'd come back to look. But whom was I kidding? With these waves, the sand was always moving. In another hour, my watch could be halfway out to sea. In a day, it could be a mile down the beach.

"I lost my watch," I sputtered to the lifeguard.

He shrugged, his way of stating the obvious: It was long gone. Ten years from now, some beachcomber with a metal detector would discover it, polished rough like sea glass. With any luck, it'd still work. As for me, I determined to do without a watch for a while. "The good Lord giveth and the good Lord taketh away," I told myself with an attempt at detachment.

For three months now I've been without a watch. Truth to tell, I haven't missed it. I've discovered that when I need to know what time it is, there are lots of clocks around. And there are times during a sermon, during a movie, during a meeting when it's just as well not to be staring at a watch. I keep thinking of a sign my seventh-grade French teacher had posted next to the clock: TIME WILL PASS. WILL YOU? I'm learning how to pay more attention to what's going on around me than on the passing time.

Lord, help me make the most of the passing years.

IT STARTS WITH A VISION

The Lord thy God will make thee plenteous in every work of thine hand, in the fruit of thy body....
—DEUTERONOMY 30:9

When our friends Scott and Katie showed us the house they had bought, my wife and I were quietly appalled. The old Victorian dowager might have been grand once, but now it was in terrible condition: plaster flaking off ceilings, windows missing panes, hardwood floors that reeked of an incontinent cat. To describe it as a fixer-upper would be generous. No matter how long I stared at the details that enchanted the new buyers—the stone fireplace, the bow windows, the leaded glass—I couldn't see how the place could be made livable.

But over time our friends succeeded mightily. They redid walls, ceilings, and floors, put in a new bathroom downstairs, fixed windows, sanded, painted, hung wallpaper. Seeing the work step by step made me appreciate how talented they were. I would never have thought of that, I'd say to myself when I saw how they opened up a room or covered up a wall. It was a kind of stewardship I could appreciate, especially since the gifts involved were foreign to me.

And then one day, when the old dowager looked completely restored, they announced to us, "We're going to move the kitchen to the other side." Both my wife and I were appalled—until we thought of what the house had first looked like.

It's a vision thing, no less essential than what it takes for a composer to write a symphony, a minister to build a church, a teacher to transform a student. They held that vision in their head as they applied their gifts to it, and when it seemed done, they were still open to a new idea. But it all had to start with a vision: to see what wasn't there. That's how it happens with the worthiest endeavors.

Lord, help me realize the visions that You put before me. Amen.

CARMEN'S GIFT

He that giveth, let him do it with simplicity....
—ROMANS 12:8

Carmen is what Victorian novelists would call simple. She can barely read, she's not very good at remembering names, and her conversation doesn't go much beyond "How are you today?" Sixty years old now, she still lives with her mother, and when she comes to church and sits in the pew, there's something of an eight-year-old about her. She alternates between rapt attention and fidgeting, her head swirling to the back of the sanctuary to see who's there, her feet swinging from the pew.

And yet, Carmen has an intuitive sense about people. When new people come to church, she makes a beeline for them at the coffee hour, grabs them by the hand, and leads them to meet people. When a parishioner has been away for a long time, she goes up to that person with a big smile and puts out her hand. When a name has been read from the pulpit with a request for prayers, she'll give whoever it is a hug later in the back of the church. I remember her best at our wedding, when she appeared at church in her prettiest party dress and shiny Mary Janes, wreathed in smiles as she celebrated our happiness.

Some people are a gift by their presence: the calming influence at a contentious meeting at work; the good listener who makes you feel better just by hearing your concerns; the enthusiast who adds energy to a room the moment she walks in the door. What is comforting about Carmen is her goodness. Her kindness arrives unedited, disarming everyone she meets. She brings out the best in people through simple warmth. That's her gift.

What can I give You, Lord? I give You my heart.

ANNIVERSARY BLESSINGS

In thee shall all families of the earth be blessed.
—GENESIS 12:3

When I came home from the office, the boys were already in the kitchen, William stirring something over the fire, Timothy pulling things out of the refrigerator. "What's for dinner?" I asked.

"You'll find out," Timothy said.

"It's a surprise," Will added.

I went into the bedroom to change clothes. My wife Carol was lounging on the bed, reading a novel—unaccustomed leisure for 6:55 on a school night. "What are they making?" I whispered.

"Ravioli, I think. With peas and a salad."

"Nice for you to get a break from cooking."

"They won't let you wash the dishes, either."

I took off my tie and removed my heavy shoes. In the dining room, Timothy was setting the table, and I could hear Will in the kitchen clanging a spoon on a pot. I thumbed through the mail and picked up a magazine. Unaccustomed leisure for me, too.

"It's done!" Will announced. "Come and get it!"

The ravioli was steamed to perfection, the peas were slathered in butter, the sauce was piping hot. My water was poured, the boys had their milk, William had lit the candles in the dining room. "Serve yourself," Timothy said proudly.

I did. We all did. Then we sat down at the dining room table. "You can say grace," Will said, and we bowed our heads.

"Dear God," I prayed, "when I got married, I never could have expected that I'd be celebrating my anniversary eighteen years later with the most perfect present. Thank you for a wonderful wife and two great kids."

"Happy anniversary!" my boys exclaimed.

Thank You, Lord, for the many blessings You've given me, especially my marriage.

WHAT 9/11 SHOWED ME

Surely goodness and mercy shall follow me all
the days of my life....
—PSALM 23:6

It's the most enduring image I have of life in New York City in those days right after 9/11. The weather, it must be remembered, was gorgeous. Clear, bright, and sunny, while smoke rose from a pit downtown. The streets near our offices on 34th Street were almost empty, making it possible for fire engines, ambulances, and emergency vehicles to rush to and from a site newly christened Ground Zero.

Posters were being put up on streetlamps with images of the missing. Little shrines of candles and flowers were assembled in parks and squares. But most of us went to our jobs, trying to do our work. At lunchtime I headed out to pick up a sandwich, and I noticed a stern-looking policeman on the corner of 33rd and Madison. That's how our police officers usually look, brusque and businesslike.

Just then a woman, clearly distraught, bumped into him. At any other time they would have backed away from each other in horror. Instead, the policeman gently put his arms on her shoulders and looked into her eyes as if to say, "Are you all right?" After a minute she nodded: "Yes, I'll be all right." And she went on her way.

It was a reminder to me that the brusque New Yorkers I live with have caring souls. Much of the time you don't know it. People are in a hurry, going about their business. But at that terrible moment we looked into each other's eyes and discovered how much goodness was there.

I shall not forget, Lord, all the goodness
You have put in Your people.

THE PRECIOUSNESS OF LIFE

To him that is joined to all the living there is hope....
—ECCLESIASTES 9:4

At first Charley thought it was carpal tunnel syndrome—
the ache in one hand and the way his fingers stopped
operating efficiently. He expected a quick diagnosis and a few
exercises; in no time he'd be back to writing long memos on
his computer for the students he taught. But the doctors' tests
dragged on for months. And the numb feeling moved up his
arm to other parts of his body. Things stopped cooperating—
his feet, his legs, his voice. When I spoke to him on the phone,
his words came out slowly, as though he were a very old man,
not the forty-five-year-old professor he was. By then the
diagnosis was in: ALS, Lou Gehrig's disease. No cure, no hope,
just a slow, irreversible deterioration.

He lived in Boston, and after receiving the news I dreaded
visiting him. It seemed incredibly sad. What would his wife
do? What about his four kids? Two sets of twins, two-year-olds
and five-year-olds. Didn't they deserve to grow up knowing the
vital, active, fun-loving man I had known? How unfair. *What's
the purpose, God?*

But that first visit with Charley surprised me. He
couldn't get up, he drawled words that had once come to
him with lightning speed, but the wit was still there. We told

stories, joked, remembered college days. And with those four children crawling all over him, darting up and down the stairs and in and out of the living room, there wasn't time to get depressed.

Later I spoke to his wife Lynn. She recalled someone visiting and telling her tearfully, "It's so sad to think of Charley dying." She looked at me sternly without a tear in her eye, "I don't see it that way, Rick. He's living. I don't know how much longer he'll be around, but every day it's life, and that's how we're getting through this."

I listened to the laughter of the children as Charley attempted to read to them. Life never seemed so precious. There was no answer to the why. Only that within the struggle, there was plenty of life left.

Lord, may I never lose my sense of how precious life is.

A SONG IN THE DARKNESS

We will sing my songs to the stringed instruments all the days of our life in the house of the Lord.
—ISAIAH 38:20

In college, Charley and I sang together in a small, all-male a cappella group. He held the baritone line with musical sureness; I was second tenor. "Melody Hamlin," he used to call me. When he and I were traveling in London with a bass, he taught us a three-part cowboy song: "Out in Arizona where the bad men are, nothing there to guide you but the evening star…"

We sang with relish, our voices echoing beneath the arches of Regent's Crescent, three singing cowboys from America. We felt right at home.

I needed a song to sing while visiting Charley. I was helping out by giving the two-year-old twins their bath, and little Nicky was having none of it. He howled. Lynn had warned me, "He gets scared of water for some reason." Fear. It seemed a perfectly reasonable reaction to life with a father who had once run races and now could barely stand. Fear of the unknown. What would Daddy be like tomorrow? How much worse would he be then? "Let's sing," I said to Nicky. Out it came, the best song I could think of: "Out in Arizona where the bad men are, nothing there to guide you but the evening star..."

Nicky looked at me, the tears slowing. I kept singing. Now he was smiling, splashing the water along with the beat: "He would moan, riding over the prairie alone, singing 'neath the Arizona sky..."

"Sing along with me," I told him. "It's a song your dad taught me." *When you sing, the future always looks better,* I thought. You can find that star to guide you 'neath the evening sky.

"I heard you," Charley drawled. "I can't sing anymore."

Of course not. He didn't have the muscle control. "It's a good song," I said. "I'll teach it to him. You taught it to me. You helped me find my way in the darkness." And helped me remember that music puts me back in touch with God.

"Sing it for me," Charley said.

I lift up my voice, Lord, and feel Your goodness.

USE MY HANDS

We then that are strong ought to bear the infirmities
of the weak....
—ROMANS 15:1

When the news of Charley's illness spread, everyone had the same response: "What can I do to help?" It was a situation that made us all feel powerless. We couldn't reverse the course of the disease; we couldn't stop Charley from dying any more than we could stop his children from growing. We could only think of little ways to help. A neighbor offered her extra bedroom so Lynn could nap whenever caregivers allowed. A friend dropped by regularly to help clean up. Parents from the kids' schools brought by meals. Charley's students did grocery shopping. Family members did carpooling. People sent cards, letters, money. Lynn learned how to ask for what she needed and to accept favors with grace.

I went to Boston for another weekend. Doing things for the kids was an obvious way to help. I read them books, made peanut-butter-and-jelly sandwiches, took them to the playground. I played games with them and taught them songs. But what could I do for Charley? By now he was largely immobile, confined to a wheelchair or bed. He could sip juice through a straw, but he couldn't raise a fork or a spoon, and chewing was an arduous process. Lynn spooned out scrambled eggs and rice for him as if she were feeding a child. Truth to tell, I was embarrassed to watch.

Then she had to get up from the table to help the kids. "Shall I?" I asked Charley timidly. He nodded. I spooned out a dollop of eggs and aimed for his mouth. It dribbled down his chin. I tried again. He strained to reach it, like a nestling stretching its neck. The third time, I landed the spoonful right in his mouth. He chewed contentedly. "You know, Charley, when we were back in college I never expected I'd be feeding you."

"You'll get better with practice," he said very slowly. I wiped his mouth with a napkin.

Lord, use my hands to serve You, however awkwardly I try.

WHEN I'M THE RICHEST

They helped every one his neighbor; and every one said to his brother, Be of good courage.
—ISAIAH 41:6

On my last visit, Charley was confined to a hospital bed set up in his living room. He had round-the-clock nursing care and was fed through a feeding tube. He could no longer speak or move more than his index finger. The easiest way to communicate with him was by selecting letters from an alphabet board. I read off the alphabet and he stopped me at the right letter by nodding yes or no. "All I'm doing is breathing," he told me. It took about twenty minutes for me to get that sentence down, one letter at a time. And yet, Charley has remained hopeful where there has been little hope. He's been faithful where others would have given up.

On this visit, I gathered around his bedside with other fellows from our college singing group. We made a quartet and sang a couple of old songs, our efforts rewarded with smiles. Someone had to cover the baritone line, Charley's part.

Lynn has saved all the letters she has received. Insurance has long since stopped covering the monumental bills for home care. Donations have come from friends and family, none of them tax-deductible. "Share the care," she calls it. She has files of correspondence from people offering prayers. The daily support network, instead of exhausting itself, has increased. The food deliveries, the volunteers who clean, take care of the kids, shop, garden. And people like my college buddies and me who have come to sing for Charley.

Here we are: a doctor, a teacher, an editor, an officer of the Federal Reserve...and a baritone with no voice or movement. All of us have asked, What purpose, God? Here we have our answer. Charley has managed to have as big an influence from where he is as any of us have from our offices or classrooms. He's brought out the best in hundreds of people, their faith, their generosity. What purpose, God? I don't know, but I do know that life is about sharing the care.

I am richest, God, when I give.

THE GATE OF LIFE IMMORTAL

Be thou faithful unto death, and I will give thee a crown of life.
—REVELATION 2:10

We got the e-mail a few weeks before Christmas: "Charley died peacefully in his sleep, surrounded by his family." We could picture the scene so well: the big hospital bed surrounded by the machines that had made Charley's last two years possible and the people who had made that life livable. Still, it seemed unbelievable that it was over. I had grown used to the thought that I could drop by the house anytime, day or night, and find Charley just inside the front door, greeting me with a smile.

We went to the service prepared for tears, buckets of them. Of course, we cried. But there were also smiles and hugs and greetings between friends who'd made Charley part of their prayers for years. It was more like a wedding than a funeral, more Easter than Good Friday. We sang the hymns that Charley had picked and listened to the verses he wanted read. We formed our own pickup choir, rehearsing before the service. "May the Lord bless you and keep you. May the Lord make His face to shine upon you." *Yes*, I thought, *God's face is shining upon everyone who has lent a hand to Charley and his family.* The church was packed with them.

The family had a reception in the parish hall afterward. We ate, laughed, and talked, the children scampering between our feet. People brought cameras to record the event. My favorite photo was of Lynn, Charley's wife, surrounded by all the daily caregivers, an indomitable bunch. Death had not triumphed here. It was "but the gate of life immortal," as one of the hymns said. At the last minute, a group of us gathered in a corner and sang one more tune for Charley: "Out in Arizona where the bad men are, nothing there to guide you but the evening star…" I drove home beneath a winter sky filled with stars.

Guide me in this life, Lord, and in the life to come.

STOPPING FOR WORSHIP
ALONG THE WAY

From one new moon to another, and from one sabbath to
another, shall all flesh come to worship before me, saith the Lord.
—ISAIAH 66:23

Summer Sundays. Wherever I am on vacation, I look for a church on a summer Sunday. Get up early, slip out before breakfast, find my way to a place I saw that had a sign out in front saying, SERVICES AT 8:00 AND 10:00. I've worshiped on a beach with my feet in the sand. I've sat in an eighteenth-century pew beneath a stark puritanical pulpit. I've sung unfamiliar songs from unfamiliar hymnals and listened to musicians on out-of-tune pianos. Sometimes I've been asked to stand up and identify myself, other times I've sat silently among the congregation. But always I've been made to feel very welcome. "New York City?" people exclaim. "You sure do need our country air!"

Indeed I do. And I need to hear different preachers give the message; big-city churches have no monopoly on good sermons. The best messages can be found in little, out-of-the-way places with only a few people in the pews. I usually look for a church of my denomination, but it's invigorating to discover one from a different tradition. Always I see the similarities shared: one faith, one Lord. What I like best, though, is being with people who believe in starting out Sunday with God. Then we scatter to the beach or the lake or the mountains.

"I'm just passing through," I explained to an elderly lady at one of the churches I visited.

"Aren't we all?" she responded wryly. How nice to stop for worship along the way.

I worship You, Lord, and praise Your name.

||||||||||||||||||||||||||||||||||||||||||||||||||||||||||||||||||||||||||||||||||||||||||||||||||||||||||||||||||||||||||

THE FAVORITE CHILD

Let there be no strife… between me and thee… for we be brethren.
—GENESIS 13:8

I've worked as an editor at Guideposts magazine for more than sixteen years, and sometimes I'm asked what my favorite story has been. I have to admit that I can't pick just one, but I can tell you about the one favorite that we never printed.

A woman from a large family hurried home to say farewell to her terminally ill father. She managed to get to the hospital just as he died. In the days that followed, all his children were home, reminiscing about their father. He had been kind, witty, and generous, and although he had nine children, he was able to make each of them feel special. It was only after the funeral that the daughter had a chance to tell her siblings what was on her mind. "I was his favorite, you know," she said. Her brothers and sisters looked at her, startled. Then they responded:

"No, I was his favorite."

"I was."

"I was."

What might have been a competition became one more shared eulogy about their dad. Each of them felt certain that he or she was the favored one. That was their father's particular gift.

It reminds me of how someone once described God: "He loves each one of us as though there were only one of us to love." If I could be as caring with my own loved ones.

There was no return address on the manuscript and the envelope it came in got lost. We could never reach the writer and therefore we could never publish the story. Perhaps someday the writer or one of her siblings will send us the story again. This time I'll be sure to save the envelope it comes in.

*Lord, give me the power to see how each of
Your children is favored by You.*

<hr/>

LEAPING AHEAD

*And ye shall hallow the fiftieth year, and proclaim liberty
throughout all the land....*
—LEVITICUS 25:10

William and David have known each other since before they could speak. We were pushing our six-month-old son Will around in a stroller when we met David in his stroller, accompanied by his parents. Ever since then it's been play dates and sleepovers, football games and basketball, e-mail, phone calls, and long rides on the school bus together. But one of the proudest moments for us to share was David's Bar Mitzvah.

At the service David stunned us with his reading in Hebrew from the Torah, the Books of Moses, and then we were further impressed by the sermon he gave, explaining the text from Leviticus 25:10, *"And ye shall hallow the fiftieth year, and proclaim liberty throughout all the land."* For a thirteen-year-old

Jewish boy, this was the moment to celebrate his coming into adulthood. For years his parents had taken him to Hebrew school, sometimes two or three times a week. But what he did with what he learned…well, that was David. His mother hinted at it in the story she told at the reception:

On a lovely summer night when David was still in his stroller, he gazed up at the sky, pointing at the crescent moon. "Cow," he said. "No," his mother responded, "moon." "Cow," David insisted. "Moon," his mother corrected. Later as she was reading him a bedtime story and looking at the illustrations, she finally understood what he was referring to: the cow that jumped over the moon. "His mind was leaping ahead of mine," she said.

That's the way it is raising children. We lead, and they leap ahead.

Lord, make me a good example to the children in my life.

||||||||||||||||||||||||||||||||||||||||||||||||||||||||||||||||||||||||||||||||||||||||||||

WELL-ORDERED PRIORITIES

Seek ye first the kingdom of God, and his righteouness;
and all these things shall be added unto you.
—MATTHEW 6:33

I was taking my younger son Timothy to school. He was worried about a test that day, and as we rode on the subway, I quizzed him on famous names from the Revolutionary War, such as Molly Pitcher, Samuel Adams, Nathan Hale. I was impressed by his knowledge. If I'd been tested, I would have struggled to come up with a definition of Thomas Paine's *Common Sense* or what battle General Burgoyne lost.

My quizzing over, I took out my pocket New Testament to do some of my own studying. In the back of my mind, I was wondering how we would fill a position at work. "Look," I said to Timothy after I had read a couple of verses, "here's a passage you know well." Seek ye first the kingdom of God, and His righteousness. He smiled. We both knew a song from church with just those words. So as the subway car was hurtling through the tunnel, stopping to let passengers on and off, both of us started singing to ourselves, "Seek ye first the kingdom of God...."

"Eighty-sixth Street," the conductor called out. Time to get off. I would drop off my son at P.S. 9, where he would define the difference between the Tories and Patriots, and I would continue on to the office, where I had to look through a pile of résumés for the right job candidate.

"Do well on the test," I said in parting.

"Do well at work," he said. We would both do fine, I decided. Our priorities were in just the right order.

Keep me focused on what is good and just and true, Lord.

‖‖

PRAYING FOR MY SPIRITUAL SIBLINGS

The Lord is nigh unto all them that call upon him... in truth.
—PSALM 145:18

The most important weekly meeting I attend at the office has no formal presentations, no overhead projectors, no budget proposals. People don't argue their positions or make impassioned justifications for their departments. Those of us who come to the conference room sit around a large table and pick up a handful of letters. In silence we read.

"My grandson needs a raise at work," a grandmother writes. "Even with overtime he's not able to support his family. Please pray for him."

"Last year I was in the hospital for five and a half weeks," says another letter. "I now have an apartment, but it does not allow pets. My twelve-and-a-half-year-old dog has been with a foster family for over a year. Please pray for me as I speak to my landlord. Wiggles is very well-behaved."

The greeting on one note makes me smile. "Hi, Spiritual Siblings!" it says. Another letter is painfully succinct: "Keep my mind intact." I find myself moved by another's plea: "I'm so lonely. I haven't met anyone who wants to date or take out a fifty-three-year-old woman. Help me to pray."

The ideal words come from a cheerful soul who says, "I live on two acres and love to mow the grass. (I have a rider.)" I read her prayer aloud: "'I have faith in Jesus. For He's there on my good days; He's there on my bad days; He's there all the time.'" What a reminder for starting out my week!

By now you might realize I'm writing about the Guideposts Prayer Fellowship. We gather in our offices on Monday mornings at 9:45 to pray for others. With every letter, I find myself fortified. It's a meeting of spiritual siblings worldwide.

Lord, be there on my good days; be there on my bad days; be there all the time.

THE MOST IMPORTANT
PART OF MY JOB

In all labour there is profit....
—PROVERBS 14:23

My first real office job came the summer after my freshman year in college. I worked in the mailroom of an architectural firm, making blueprints, photocopying, binding specs, wrapping packages, and taking them to the post office. In two days I figured I had mastered everything. "There's not much else to learn," I said to my dad.

"Try learning people's names," he suggested.

That took another week, matching the faces with names and knowing where everybody sat. Just when I thought I'd mastered that, Dad asked, "What do you know about their jobs? How about their families? Do you know their kids' names and what they do?" This was a whole new assignment. On my rounds I began to study family photographs and ask a few questions. There was a lot to absorb.

"I hear people make suggestions about what we can do better in the office," I said.

"Good," Dad said enthusiastically. "Pass on what you hear to your boss."

That took a lot of courage, but I did it, and my boss seemed appreciative. Then, at the end of summer, I heard someone praise the work of another colleague. "Pass that along, too," Dad said. "You can never do wrong by passing along praise."

The job ended with a handshake and a check. The money disappeared very fast, along with my knowledge of how to make a blueprint. But what I discovered about working in an office has lasted. Learn people's names, find out more about them, listen to what they say, and never, ever hesitate to pass along some words of praise.

Thanks, Dad.

Help me see in my work, Lord, that caring for other people
is the most important part of the job.

‖‖

SERVING GOD WHERE I AM

I will restore health unto thee, and I will heal thee of
thy wounds, saith the Lord.
—JEREMIAH 30:17

The news from home had me worried. Dad was in the hospital for a torn Achilles tendon. After surgery he wouldn't be able to walk for six weeks. I could picture him trapped upstairs in the bedroom, Mom shuttling up and down, taking him his meals, mail, newspaper. If I were closer to home, at least I could run errands for her, or help Dad with his physical therapy. But they were in California, some two thousand miles away, so I had to content myself with phone calls and letters. What else could I do?

Then my friend Gary had a seizure. He lives in an apartment across the street. The doctors weren't sure what the cause was, but they didn't want him going to work on his own. "Rick," he asked me one evening on the phone, "could you accompany me on the subway in the morning? My doctor doesn't want me to be alone, in case I have another seizure."

"Sure," I said. "No problem."

The next day I met Gary outside his building and we walked to the station together. "I know you like to pray in the mornings," he said, "so go ahead. I have something to read." On the train I took out my Bible and he took out his newspaper. When I closed my eyes, I had a lot on my mind. *Lord, be with Mom and Dad back home. I wish I could be there.* Then it occurred to me that God had given me something good to do right here. *Be with Gary as the doctors help him.*

Later when I talked to Mom, she told me about all the people who had been giving them a hand. "I'm sorry I can't be with you," I said.

"That's all right," she said. "I know there are things you need to be doing there." Someday I'd tell her the half of it.

Let me serve You, Lord, wherever I am.

SUMMER BLACKOUT!

When thou hast eaten and art full, then thou shalt bless the Lord thy God for the good land which he hath given thee.
—DEUTERONOMY 8:10

A summer blackout. New York is famous for them. People trapped in elevators, subways, high-rise office buildings in the sweltering heat. When one happened last year, we were lucky. We were trapped at home with plenty of flashlights and candles. "It's kind of nice," I said to my wife Carol, "the quiet, without everyone's air conditioners running." Neighbors poured out of their apartments and congregated on the sidewalk, exchanging information. How long would the power be out? What had caused it? How far did the blackout area extend?

Back inside, I opened the refrigerator to get something to drink. Why is the light out? I wondered, and then remembered. Of course, the power outage! I wandered over to the computer. No, that wouldn't work. Nor would the television. If I could listen to a little music on my CD player...impossible. Absentmindedly I flicked the switch for the ceiling fan. I would lie in bed and stay cool—but naturally the fan wouldn't work, either. I opened the windows wide, grateful for the breeze. Just then Carol came into the bedroom. "There's not much water coming out of the faucet," she said. Of course—the pumps run on electricity.

That night I read in bed by flashlight, feeling like a kid on a camping trip. The next morning, as I sadly emptied soured milk down the drain, I was grateful for official promises of power by midday. (I could only read about it in the newspaper.)

Sometimes you don't realize how good things are until they go. For the time being I thanked God for sunshine, candlelight, batteries, and the breeze. And I would never take a glass of cold water for granted again.

Thank You, Lord, for my well-fed life. Forgive me
for taking it for granted.

SPIRITUAL ENEMIES

Deliver me from mine enemies, O my God: defend me
from them that rise up against me.
—PSALM 59:1

There are verses of the Bible that I would rather skip, whole passages that I would like to believe simply don't apply to me and my modern-day circumstances. "These words probably meant something to believers hundreds of years ago," I tell myself, "but for me, they don't count." The verses I stumble over are the ones that ask for God's vengeance, like this from the Fifty-ninth Psalm: "Consume them in wrath, consume them that they may not be."

"I don't have any enemies," I said to a friend. "Or at least not enemies on whom I would wish such harm." I like to consider myself a mild-mannered, easygoing person.

"Okay," my friend said, "maybe you don't know any people you'd wish vengeance upon, but what about spiritual enemies? Do you have any of them?"

"Sure," I said. "Things like sloth, envy, anger, pride. They drive me nuts."

"Spoken honestly," he said. "Then look at the Psalms as your chance to ask God to wreak havoc on them. The language is strong because that's just how we should speak to our enemies. Especially spiritual ones."

So I went back to the Fifty-ninth Psalm and looked back at passages like, "Let them make a noise like a dog and go round about the city. Let them wander up and down for meat, and grudge if they be not satisfied." How about that for sloth? Why not that for pride? Strong words for some terrible foes— and just what they deserve. The Psalmist knew exactly what he was doing. Some things we shouldn't be mild-mannered about.

Consume my spiritual enemies, Lord, that they may not be.

||||||||||||||||||||||||||||||||||||||||||||||||||||||||||||||||||||||||||||||||||||||||||||||||||||||||||||||||||||||||||||||||

THE COMMUNITY OF PRAYER

*I have called daily upon thee, I have stretched out
my hands unto thee.*
—PSALM 88:9

My wife Carol has a group of friends on the Internet, most of whom she's never met face-to-face. They are part of a network set up by our college where alumni from different classes get to know each other. In her group the primary bond is parenting—all of the alums are rearing children—and over the years they have come to know one another well, discussing everything from homework problems to soccer camp. Inevitably, they have also talked each other through some tough times.

One of the toughest came when one member was diagnosed with breast cancer. Advice flew through cyberspace—what treatments to try, what doctors had said, which hospitals were best. In this case, the family made the decision to move across the country to be near a fine hospital in Texas. Progress reports kept the e-mail group well informed. But then, at a crucial moment, someone came up with an idea as good as any medical science had provided. "12:00 tomorrow, Central Time, let's meet for prayer," said the e-mail message.

The next day Carol logged on at 1:00 our time, noon in Texas, and opened her e-mail. She scrolled down. "I'm here," "Ready," "Waiting," came the litany of responses, and from office buildings in New York to kitchens in California, people prayed through the great electronic silence. "Amen," they signed out.

No one who first heard Christ say, "Where two or more are gathered in my name," could have guessed at a gathering encompassing thousands of miles. But then again, the mystery and power of prayer is more profound than cyberspace. And our communities of prayer need only be a password away.

May I be tireless, Lord, in Your community of prayer.

CAUSE FOR CELEBRATION

All the ends of the world shall remember and turn unto the Lord.
—PSALM 22:27

April 19 is an important anniversary for me. I like to celebrate it with my friend Ray, because it's important for him, too. He calls me or I call him and we schedule lunch. Initially we don't talk about why we happen to be celebrating. Maybe I'll be conscious of it in a noisy restaurant as I try to seat myself close to his right side because he's been deaf in his left ear since his operation. Or I might scratch my left ear and think of it because of the lingering numbness in my nerves there ever since my operation. Otherwise we talk about our kids, our wives, our work.

At the end of lunch, when I'm taking a bite out of his slice of chocolate cake and he's taking a spoonful of my apple pie, it will come up in an oblique way. I'll remember that morning when we were both recovering from surgery, when the best distraction from my discomfort had been to pray for him because I was too afraid to pray for myself. That we both had tumors in similar places and that we both were operated on—in different hospitals—on the same day was the sort of coincidence that we would have been happier without.

But then came the good news. My surgery was successful, so was his. Both our tumors were benign. In the five years since, our other news has been good. So we schedule this annual lunch to remind ourselves of our blessings. We have a lot to be grateful for. No one knows that as well as Ray and I, two guys in business suits at a thanksgiving feast. Just what an anniversary is for.

Let me never forget all the good reasons I have
for celebrating, Lord!

WHAT GRACE IS

Ye all are partakers of my grace.
—PHILIPPIANS 1:7

I was cleaning out my son William's desk on a Saturday afternoon, while wondering how I would manage the next day's lesson with his Sunday school class. As I went through drawers of old party favors, homework assignments, worn-out pencils, forgotten cards, I asked myself, "How will I explain grace to these kids? It's a little like having your mom or dad clean up your room when you're not home," I grumbled on. "You should do it yourself, but they do it because they love you."

Well, what good is grace then? That was just the sort of question one of my charges would ask. What would I tell him?

Then I had a very clear vision, a memory from childhood: coming home from school with a heavy book bag and walking into my bedroom to see everything spotless because Mom had cleaned and reorganized my desk. I should have done it, but she did it, and I was all too grateful.

"When grace is given to you, you feel more inclined to extend it to others as best you can," I answered my own question.

Or to take William's words when he saw his room all clean, "You spoil me, Dad."

"I have been spoiled myself," I told him.

Lord, as I have been given, let me give.

EASTER'S MESSAGE

God will redeem my soul from the power of the grave: for he shall receive me....
—PSALM 49:15

That fall morning it was brisk outside, the first really cold day of the season. I glanced at the thermometer in the window: thirty-nine degrees. I turned to the newspaper for the forecast: it wouldn't even get up to fifty. Time for the winter wardrobe. I searched the back of the closet for my tweed jacket. Brown with autumnal highlights of gold and red, it was the perfect thing for an October day.

As I walked to the train, I took a look at the garden in front of our apartment. The hydrangeas were turning copper, the mums a brave yellow, and the little Japanese maple at the end of the drive had already blushed red. Soon there would be no flowers, no leaves, and the only bit of color would be the big red bow on the wreaths put up at Christmastime. I found myself yearning for spring.

I put my hands in my jacket. When did I last wear it? Probably last winter or on one of the cold days of early spring. But what a difference there is between a cold October day, when the summer is past, and a day in March, when spring is just around the bend. There's something sad about saying good-bye to those vibrant colors when they won't be back for six months.

Then I felt something in my pocket and took it out. A dried palm branch woven in the shape of a cross. I suddenly remembered the last time I wore this jacket: Palm Sunday. That day in church, as I listened to the extraordinary story of Christ's suffering, I wove this cross from a green palm frond. Then Easter came with its bright promise of everlasting life, and soon spring followed. I put the cross back in my jacket and kept it there. Easter has a message I need all year long.

Lord, I turn to You for the promise of new life.

THANKSGIVING JOYS

Offer unto God thanksgiving....
—PSALM 50:14

It seems to take hours for everybody to get seated on Thanksgiving. The steaming mashed potatoes fog up people's glasses, the stuffing spills off the serving platter, the dish of cranberry sauce gets passed around, there's a request for salt and pepper from one end of the table—sometimes two tables in our cramped dining room. And then, something that's a tradition in our house: There's a clink of a spoon against a glass for silence. "Pam, do you want to start?" I ask. Pam, an old friend, is good at setting the mood.

"I'd like to say how grateful I am for my mother and what she gave me when I was growing up," she begins. The opportunity is passed around the table, just like that dish of cranberry sauce. From five-year-olds to ninety-five-year-olds, everyone gets to express what they're thankful for. The litany is wide-ranging, from a winning soccer season and the life of a pet rabbit to good health. Tears well up behind the fogged glasses. The teenagers roll their eyes at first, then rise in eloquence to the occasion. I start worrying that the succotash is growing cold and the pie will burn in the oven. But blessings must be said. We are a group of many faiths, and one or two with no declared faith at all. But thanksgiving runs deep.

Lord, I'm thankful for this day when thankfulness is on everyone's lips.

A SURE HOPE

Hope we have as an anchor of the soul, both sure and steadfast....
—HEBREWS 6:19

One hundred tulip bulbs shipped from a gardening company in the Midwest. Ever since I ordered those first hundred bulbs a couple of years ago, the company has had my number. They send me catalogs every fall and then a reminder in the form of a postcard that asks, "Have you ordered your spring bulbs yet?" I fill out the card and send it in. The bulbs, they promise, will arrive at the seasonally and regionally appropriate moment for planting.

I leave them in the refrigerator for a couple of weeks, making sure that Indian summer has passed. Then, on a bitter December day when others are putting up wreaths and hanging lights, I put in my bulbs. In the weak sunlight, with dead leaves blowing past, I dig into the cold earth and think about where the purple, yellow, and scarlet-tinged flowers will look best. I can see them in my mind's eye, just like the photo in the catalog, even though the box hedge is bare and the hydrangeas are sticks. The Christmas carols will be sung and the stockings hung, but I'll be thinking about my bulbs. They give me hope through the snow and ice and frozen mud. Beneath it new life is growing.

I don't mind waiting for things—good dinners with friends, a new book by a favorite author, a movie with an unbeatable cast—as long as I know they're coming. I say the prayers of Advent and think of my tulips. I can weather any winter storm as long as I've made that down payment on spring.

Lord, I trust You with my hopes. May they grow.

SAVOR EACH DAY

And the shepherds returned, glorifying and praising God for
all the things that they had heard and seen....

—LUKE 2:20

There comes that time on Christmas Day when all the gifts are given, brunch is consumed, the guests have left, and there is nothing more to unwrap. In my family we go to our little stockpile of presents and take a mental inventory. Who was it that gave me that nice blue sweater? That tie will go well with my brown suit. I must tell my parents that the towels are perfect. The boys inspect their books while Carol fantasizes about a recipe in her new cookbook. Then as I put on the CD I was given, Timothy looks up from his new board game. "Dad, do you want to play Risk?" he asks.

"Sure," I say. William joins us for the game, as Carol settles in with the novel that her sister sent. We roll the dice and are soon absorbed in strategizing over the territory on the Risk board. As I listen to the music and hear Carol turn pages in her book (and listen to Timothy agonize over how to conquer Asia), I think about how grateful I am to have this family, to have this apartment for a home, to have friends and family who care enough about me to send gifts.

It's not the presents that have made this a fine Christmas Day. It's this time together, lounging on a winter's afternoon. It's being able to savor it without having to rush to the office or read my e-mail. It's hearing Carol chuckle in the armchair and watching the boys beat their dear old dad. Sure enough, busyness will return, but this day has reminded me of all the things I have that can't be wrapped up. That feels like my holiday gift. And for that I thank the good Lord.

Dear God, let me savor every day as though it were Christmas.

||||||||||||||||||||||||||||||||||||||||||||||||||||||||||||||||||||||||||||||||||||||||||||||||||||||||||||||||||||||||||||||||||

THE GIFT OF CREATIVITY

He that giveth, let him do it with simplicity....
—ROMANS 12:8

It used to make me so frustrated. As a child, whenever I asked my dad what he wanted for Christmas, he said, "Just give me a hug and a kiss." And when I asked my mom, she said, "Why don't you make something nice?" It didn't seem fair because when I went to the stores clutching the few quarters in my pocket, I could spot all sorts of things that looked a lot nicer than any picture I could draw. I admired a vase all shiny and pink, and there was a framed picture of a forest with trees that, unlike mine, really looked like trees. And if I had enough money I could buy my dad something really useful, like socks or a new belt.

Alas, I didn't have enough money, so instead I made a dog out of clay that could work as a paperweight, and another year I made a tissue-paper collage of angels singing "Hark, the Harold Angels Sing!" (spelled just like that) and crafted an ornament out of papier-mâché that had a miniature Nativity scene inside. These I dispensed with hugs and kisses, but I couldn't help thinking those items from Woolworth's would have been more impressive gifts. Maybe when I was older I could buy Mom a scarf and Dad some handkerchiefs.

Since then I've been able to afford belts and handkerchiefs and scarves and the proverbial new tie that my father always requests, but when I go home at Christmastime it's the handmade gifts that are still displayed: the "Harold Angels" singing, the papier-mâché Nativity scene, the paperweight pooch. It's not just that they came from the heart, but they also came from the hand. That's why I tell my own children, "Make me something nice." A gift of creativity is meant to be shared. It can last forever.

Thank You, God, for the gift of creativity. Help me share mine.

‖‖‖

NO NEED TO FEAR

Behold, the angel of the Lord appeared unto him in a dream,
saying, Joseph, thou son of David, fear not to take
unto thee Mary thy wife....
—MATTHEW 1:20

Carol was six months pregnant with our first child that December, the year we saw Advent through new eyes.

When I sat in the pew and heard Bible lessons about waiting, I wondered what our child would be like. What sort of gifts would he have? Who would he take after in our family? As an expectant father I had my own set of worries: Would I be able to make enough to support a child? Would I be patient enough as a father? What if I had a kid who wanted to play catch every night? I was terrible at baseball.

After the service people would smile at Carol and say to me, "Aren't you excited about having a baby?" Scared to death was more like it. Then, one Sunday, the lesson was about Joseph and how he was ready to walk away from Mary when he discovered she was pregnant until an angel in a dream reassured him, "Fear not." The rest he had to take on trust. The trip to Bethlehem, the visits from wise men and shepherds, the hurried escape to Egypt—the Christmas story wouldn't have happened if Joseph hadn't trusted God.

So I promised I would trust God.

When William was born, I managed to find the energy to get up in the middle of the night when I had to, and in those first few years of parenthood we were always able to pay the bills. When he grew old enough to want to throw a ball after school, I learned how to throw one, too. Now as he enters his fourteenth year, I confess I have a whole new set of worries. What if he falls in with the wrong set of kids in high school? What if I can't afford college? What if he does poorly on his entrance exams? Then I remember: "Fear not." It's a gift I could use every Advent.

Thank You, God, for the gift of faith.

GRANDMA'S FINAL GIFT

Every man shall give as he is able....
—DEUTERONOMY 16:17

My mother-in-law was an alcoholic. She loved her grandchildren, but her addiction made it hard to express that love. Every fall, for a dozen years, we went through the same heartbreaking scenario. In September she would call Carol and ask, "What can I get the boys for Christmas?" Carol gave her mother lists of things the boys liked and sent her samples from catalogs. She went so far as to suggest an 800 number to call with the exact item number of the Lego or Playmobil toy or football jersey.

Finally, about a week before Christmas we would get another call. "I'm so sorry," my mother-in-law would say, "I just haven't had time to get anything for the boys. Let me send you a check. You get something nice and put my name on it." Because we wanted the boys to know their grandmother loved them, we obliged. But it was painful.

Then one summer she did something very brave. She went into a rehab program and stopped drinking. That fall there were no calls from my mother-in-law about what the boys wanted for Christmas. No matter. We were busy rejoicing in her recovery. What we didn't know is that her body hadn't really recovered from the ravages of her disease. After only three months of sobriety, she had a massive stroke and died two days before Thanksgiving.

That December was a sad one, full of regrets. What if she had stopped drinking earlier? What if we had urged her into rehab years ago? We asked ourselves a thousand "what ifs?" Then, before Christmas, a big package arrived in the mail. Carol looked quizzically at the return address. It wasn't from a mail-order company she knew, and a phone call to California assured her that it hadn't come from my family. When she opened the box she discovered a present for the boys, ordered by their grandmother. The one present my mother-in-law had bought before she died. A gift that meant more than words can tell.

Lord, help me give in return for all I have received.

THE PERFECT PRESENT

They presented unto him gifts; gold, and
frankincense, and myrrh.
—MATTHEW 2:11

The anxiety begins just after Thanksgiving, about the time all the stores put up their Christmas decorations and the first Christmas cards arrive. I start asking myself, What will I get Carol for Christmas?

Let me make something clear here: We're not big spenders at Christmas. It's not the small box from Tiffany's or the big one from Saks that she would like or I would consider. The commercialism of the season appalls me. That said, I'm a late convert to gift giving. The joke goes around the office, "So, Rick, what are you going to get Carol? Another frying pan? A pot holder?" One of my best friends once bought his wife a new hubcap for Christmas. A hubcap! She wasn't exactly thrilled.

What both my friend and I have learned is that a gift is only right when it shows how much you've thought about the recipient and consider what really pleases her. So at Christmastime I go into places I know nothing about: a store that only sells soap, a hand-thrown pottery shop, a boutique filled with beautiful scarves. I cringe when a salesperson discovers my ignorance. But that's part of the process— learning about things my wife likes.

You might say it's the thought that counts. I'd go further than that. The wise men traveled hundreds of miles to give the Christ Child gold, frankincense, and myrrh. I take a subway, a bus, and clippings of ideas I've culled throughout the year. The right present has a long journey attached to it. One that puts you in the ranks of those who realized that a little child could be an uncrowned king.

Lord, give me patience and understanding
at this gift-giving time of year.

WHO IT'S ALL ABOUT

Ye are all the children of light, and the children of the day....
—I THESSALONIANS 5:5

Why is it that at the busiest time of year choir directors and congregations expect ten times more singing than any other month? For us choristers, it means that on top of shopping and card writing and wrapping, there are extra rehearsals and services. I tell myself this is pleasurable. The music is beautiful, and the people who hear it will be inspired, calmed, transported. But there's a point in the rehearsals when I grumble, "Never again."

I was close to that point recently when our choir director said in exasperation after we sang the same thing for about the tenth time, "Softer. More intense. Make it really musical." We went over the passage again, and from the look on his face, we weren't any better.

That's when Willis, a soft-spoken tenor, raised his hand and said, "I always remember something my music professor once said to me: 'Don't wake the baby.'"

We laughed. After all, Willis's wife was due to have a baby any moment. The image seemed just right. It helped us nail that passage of music. And it gave me what I was looking for as I went through the rest of the holiday season. *The Baby. It's all about the Baby!*

> *Lord, You came to the world as a child so that we might greet You with childlike wonder.*

||||||||||||||||||||||||||||||||||||||||||||||||||||||||||||||||||||||||||||||||||||||||||||||||||||||

THE CHRISTMAS ELF

> *For unto you is born this day in the city of David a Saviour, which is Christ the Lord.*
> —LUKE 2:11

The gifts began arriving on the first of December. Little things that appeared in unexpected places. A Christmas ornament, small Nativity figures, candy, oranges, a short booklet of devotions. And with each gift came a note, sometimes with a Bible verse, sometimes with a typed word of appreciation, and always signed, "Your Christmas elf." My friends Jim and Wendy didn't know who the giver was, but soon their children were peeking out of windows, hoping to catch the elf in the act.

It would have been easy to find the elf if he or she left the gifts at the front door in broad daylight, but this elf was secretive. The first arrived in the still of the night to be discovered with the morning paper. Others appeared on a desk at the office, on a car seat in the church parking lot, and even in a nursery-school cubby. "Who do you think it is?" they asked each other every evening. It had to be someone who knew them well enough to put the gifts where Jim and Wendy would discover them. And it was someone who appreciated all Jim and Wendy had done for their community.

Finally, on Christmas Eve, Wendy figured it out. She found her clue in the minister's message: "Christmas arrives in the still of the night with little warning. A stable, a small provincial town, an undistinguished couple. The greatest gift of all hardly called any attention to itself. God's own Son born in a manger."

"It was you!" Wendy exclaimed to her pastor after the service.

"How'd you guess?" he responded, as he sheepishly fished the final present out of his pocket, a figure of the Baby Jesus in the manger for the Nativity.

"Your sermon," she said. "It gave you away." But as she thought about it, his giving in secret was the sermon. "Merry Christmas," she said.

"Merry Christmas!"

Father, prepare my heart for the gift of Your Son.

THE BEST GIFT I CAN GIVE

What shall I render unto the Lord for all his benefits toward me?
—PSALM 116:12

Christmas Eve came almost three weeks after my heart surgery. I was thrilled to be back at church, delighted to see so many dear friends after the rigors of hospitalization. The minister even announced that I was present. I rose to my feet, my hands in my pockets and a scarf wrapped around my neck to keep me warm, and received a round of applause. I waved to my cohorts in the balcony where for countless Christmas Eves

I'd sung with the choir. It sounded like they were managing fine without me.

Sharing a hymnal with my son, I was having a little trouble singing. No doctor had warned me about this. They said it would take a while before I would be walking at a quick pace or running or going to the gym, but they didn't tell me that my breath for singing would go wonky on every other note. I'd sing a phrase and then have to rest to sing the next one. One venerable carol after another, and I was only half present, if that. Usually we like to divide parts as a family and harmonize together. Well, I was pretty useless. *How can I celebrate Christmas if I can't sing?*

Then we came to one of my favorite carols, "In the Bleak Midwinter," and I wanted to throw down the book at the ugly croaking I was making. But there in the last verse was the message I needed to hear: "What can I give him, poor as I am?" The answer from Christina Rossetti, the lyricist: "Give him my heart." Nothing more, nothing less. I didn't have to sing a stirring tenor descant from the loft. All I needed to do was love and be loved.

What I can give, Lord, I give: my heart, my self.

A NOTE FROM
THE EDITORS

We hope you enjoy *101 Moments in the Presence of God*, created by the Books and Inspirational Media Division of Guideposts, a nonprofit organization. In all of our books, magazines and outreach efforts, we aim to deliver inspiration and encouragement, help you grow in your faith, and celebrate God's love in every aspect of your daily life.

Thank you for making a difference with your purchase of this book, which helps fund our many outreach programs to the military, prisons, hospitals, nursing homes and schools. To learn more, visit GuidepostsFoundation.org.

We also maintain many useful and uplifting online resources. Visit Guideposts.org to read true stories of hope and inspiration, access OurPrayer network, sign up for free newsletters, download free e-books, join our Facebook community, and follow our stimulating blogs.

To learn about other Guideposts publications, including the best-selling devotional *Daily Guideposts*, go to ShopGuideposts.org, call (800) 932-2145 or write to Guideposts, PO Box 5815, Harlan, Iowa 51593.